The Murder of Cara Knott

Jessi Dilmont

Published by Trellis Publishing, 2021.

While every precaution has been taken in the preparation of this book, the publisher assumes no responsibility for errors or omissions, or for damages resulting from the use of the information contained herein.

THE MURDER OF CARA KNOTT

First edition. July 3, 2021.

Copyright © 2021 Jessi Dilmont.

ISBN: 979-8224027859

Written by Jessi Dilmont.

THE MURDER OF CARA KNOTT

JESSI DILMONT

1

Three decades after a murder that shook the city of San Diego to its core, residents and visitors are still reminded of the tragic slaying each time they drive down Interstate 15. Near Mercy Road, where 20 year old San Diego State junior Cara Knott was killed in 1986, hangs a sign that reads "Knott Memorial Bridge."

The killing was difficult enough for the community to swallow – a young, beautiful woman, full of potential, never even lives to see her college graduation. But what made the murder even more horrifying was the arrest that soon followed. California Highway Patrol officer Craig Peyer, who had pulled the student over as she'd been driving home, was charged with killing Cara Knott.

California highways were a dangerous place for women in the decades leading up to Knott's death. Stories of women being abducted, assaulted, or killed at the side of the road were everywhere, and it wasn't unusual for a missing girl to turn up murdered in a California ditch. In 1986, women were afraid of pulling over onto poorly-lit shoulders, alone and vulnerable.

At Peyer's sentencing, Supreme Court Judge Richard Huffman said the officer "took advantage of a position of trust and confidence."

"It terrorized everybody," recalled Paul Pfingst, who'd handled Peyer's retrial in the late 1980s after the first trial resulted in a deadlocked jury. "I have never seen a case that has such a direct impact on people's perception of their safety, especially women. It popped the bubble of perceived safety."

Peyer was found guilty of murder by the jury at the second trial, with the verdict handed down June 22, 1988. In June 2018, 30 years after the jury announced its decision, Knott's mother, Joyce, said she hadn't even been aware of the unfortunate anniversary.

"I think of the dates that have to do with her," she told a reporter with the San Diego Union Tribune, "not that have to do with the trial."

A typical drive home

On December 27, 1986, Cara Knott had been visiting her boyfriend in Escondido. She called her parents shortly after 8 o'clock that evening, letting them know that she'd be on her way back to their El Cajon home shortly. It was a 45 minute drive, and one Knott made quite frequently.

But she never made it back home.

By 10 p.m., when his daughter still hadn't arrived, Sam Knott was overwhelmed by the feeling that she was in danger. He and his wife, Joyce, set out to search for Knott along Interstate 15, the road she usually took between the family's home and her boyfriend's.

As the clock ticked closer to midnight, Sam was becoming increasingly concerned for his daughter's well being. He signalled to a passing highway patrol car and asked the officer to put out an all-points alert for Knott, but was informed that there was nothing the authorities could do until she'd been gone for at least 24 hours. So, Sam and Joyce began their own search – spending the night canvassing the county's freeways and off-ramps, as well as darkened shopping malls and parking lots. But they didn't stop calling the police. During one of Sam's impassioned pleas for help, the dispatcher calmly responded, "girls will be girls."

Knott's sister Cynthia and her brother-in-law Bill Weick, who'd spent the night searching along with Knott's parents, decided at around 5:30 a.m. to venture a little further down an off-ramp at Mercy Road. The road hadn't yet been completed, so it came to an end in a shadowy pit underneath the busy interstate.

"It was foggy and dark and creepy," Weick testified, months later, "like something out of a movie."

As they proceeded slowly past the construction roadblocks, they found Knott's distinctive vehicle. The 1968 Volkswagen Beetle was empty below I-15 at Mercy Road, abandoned near a bridge along the frontage road. The keys were still in the ignition, a credit card was left lying on the driver's seat, and her overnight bag was still sitting in the backseat. Knott, though, had seemingly disappeared.

Panicked, the couple began frantically searching the immediate area – calling Knott's name over and over again before finally reaching out to the police for help. Meanwhile, Sam was speeding down I-15 himself, pursuing a black and white police car with his lights flashing in an attempt to catch the officer's eye. He continued to follow the cruiser as it turned off the freeway onto the Mercy Road exit, and was shocked to see his daughter and his son-in-law waiting near Knott's empty car.

Sam, Cynthia, and Bill were combing the area with police at 8:12 that morning, when Cara Knott's body was found less than a mile away from her car – dumped about 75 feet to the ground below. She'd been strangled before being thrown from the bridge.

"This was one of the most intense investigations I've ever been involved with," said San Diego homicide lieutenant Phil Jarvis, who eventually put three times the typical number of technicians and detectives to work on the case.

What was particularly troubling for Jarvis was Knott's motive. Why had she stopped her car on a cold winter night on an unfinished road that didn't lead anywhere? Time of death had been determined to be sometime between 9 and 10 p.m., and a receipt from a Chevron gas station indicated she'd refuelled at 8:27. The vehicle was working fine, and the passenger-side door was still locked – Cara Knott hadn't been the type to pick up hitchhikers, her family said. There was no sign of a struggle, either.

However, despite the cold weather – one of the coldest nights of the year – her driver-side window was left partly rolled down. To investigators, it seemed like Knott had pulled over for someone she trusted – someone like a police officer.

"Did you choke her?"

The very next day, as the story got out to the news media, a TV reporter contacted California Highway Patrol and asked to interview an officer about what women could do to stay safe while traveling alone at night. She was put in touch with Peyer, who answered her questions, during a ride along on camera, with fresh scratches on his face.

"You never know who you could meet along the road ... Anything could happen," he said to Rory Devine, the reporter with NBC San Diego who went with him on the ride-along. "Being a female, you could be raped, robbed if you're a male, all the way where you could be killed."

It only took a week before the homicide investigative team began looking at Peyer as a potential suspect, despite his clean record and thirteen years with the California Highway Patrol. But evidence linked him to the case – blood and fibers found on Knott's body, and a witness who'd seen Peyer pull Knott over on the evening she was killed.

The scratches on Peyer's face had also aroused suspicion. According to the story Peyer had given, they'd been the result of a fall into a fence lining the parking lot of the California Highway Patrol, but upon further investigation, the fence was determined to be too high up to create the scratches on Peyer's face. Additionally, reports had been collected from witnesses who thought they'd seen Peyer at a gas station around the time of the murder, screaming into the parking lot at high speed and looking troublingly disheveled.

One of the witnesses, an off-duty officer with the San Diego police department, had noticed the scratches on Peyer's face – approximately one hour before Peyer claimed he'd fallen into the fence.

Then, more women came forward with stories of their own, describing Peyer's behaviour when he'd similarly pulled them over, as well. Nearly two dozen calls came in to the department, with the mainly female callers recounting stories of being pulled over by Peyer on that same off-ramp – and, although Peyer hadn't been violent or hostile to any of the women in these cases, he'd certainly left an impression.

While the women claimed Peyer had been relatively friendly, his behaviour had made them feel uncomfortable. Some callers reported that they'd been especially bothered by the way he had gently run his hands along their hair and shoulders. In fact, several complaints had been made about Peyer prior to Knott's murder, but because of Peyer's many years of service and glowing reputation within the department, they'd been simply dismissed.

Then, a witness claimed to have seen a Volkwagen Beetle, assumed to be the car Knott had been driving, accompanied by a marked highway patrol car at the time and place where the murder was thought to have occurred. The last time Knott had been seen alive was only two miles from the place where her body was found, at a Chevron gas station. And the attendant on duty could clearly recall spotting a car marked "California Highway Patrol" pull a U-turn in front of the station just as Knott was driving out of the parking lot.

Peyer's alibi was also determined to be false. His logbook was filled with inaccurate documentation around the time Knott had been killed, and he'd made several changes to traffic tickets he'd issued in the hours after the murder – as noted by the motorists who'd been given the tickets that night. One citation had been handed out with the time of 9:20 written overtop of a scratched out 10:30, issued the night Cara Knott was killed by officer Peyer.

A rope found in Peyer's patrol car was examined by forensic dentist Norman Sperber, who concluded that it appeared to match the marks found around Knott's neck – although later, Sperber would be barred from presenting this evidence in court. A distinctive fiber had been found on Knott's dress, a specific type of gold rayon made by using a yellow pigment rather than a dye, and was the same kind of fabric used on the shoulder patch of Peyer's highway patrol uniform. The microscopic purple fibers found on Knott's body could also be traced back to Peyer.

More specifically, though, a small drop of blood had been discovered on one of the boots Knott had been wearing. The blood type was determined to be AB negative – the rarest type, but consistent with Peyer's. Other genetic markers were also found, but at the time of the investigation, technology was not available for DNA testing to provide conclusive results.

Officers who worked with Peyer testified that he'd begun acting strangely after the murder – frequently requesting updates regarding the status of the investigation, and making repeated attempts to rationalize that the perpetrator's crime was nothing more than a simple mistake. And after an internal investigation at California Highway Patrol was completed, it was revealed that while many of the drivers Peyer had stopped were pulled over for legitimate violations, an overwhelming majority were young women, driving alone – women of a similar age group and physical appearance as Cara Knott.

Peyer's colleagues with the highway patrol knew him as a "hot pencil," who issued up to 250 traffic citations each month. The area around Mercy Road had been a part of his patrol since 1982 – in fact, after the discovery of Knott's body in the area, one of the officers teased, "What happened, Craig, did you choke her for not signing a ticket?"

"Breaking his sacred trust"

Even with the evidence piling up against him, however, it wasn't enough to unanimously convince a jury. The first trial deadlocked with a 7-5 split, with the jury leaning more toward a conviction. So, with another trial looming, the family requested a new prosecutor. And Pfingst, who'd recently moved to San Diego from New York, was up for the challenge.

He told the jury that Peyer's "predatory nature" led him to stop young women driving alone, then order them down the isolated frontage road from the Mercy Road off-ramp – where Knott's body had been found. He posited that, perhaps, Knott and Peyer had engaged in some sort of altercation before Peyer, afraid that the young woman would go to the police, strangled her and threw her from the bridge.

Peyer's darker side was revealed to the court during the course of the trials, as well as in a probation report that had been compiled by the agency following his conviction. According to a probation officer, one of the two women who'd previously been married to Peyer had claimed that after he joined the highway patrol, he started acting like "Mr. Macho," and treated his bad as "a way to flirt."

At the trial, more than 20 young women provided testimony describing how Peyer had pulled them over at night for minor traffic violations – in the same isolated area where Knott's body had been found. According to many of these women, who were eventually allowed to drive away without even a citation, Peyer kept them detained on the desolate off-ramp for an hour and a half or more, asking intrusive questions about their personal lives.

"He just seemed like a lonely guy, bored with his shift," said a woman Peyer had pulled over just a few months before Knott's murder. "He leaned against my car just making chitchat, asking me lots of questions about myself ... I think he liked pulling young women over and being the authority figure. He was a gentleman, but the longer he kept me down there, the more nervous I got."

The jury spent days deliberating the case before finally coming back with a verdict. Knott's mother, Joyce, cried as the foreman announced that Peyer had been found guilty of Knott's murder.

"Words cannot express our emotions," she said. "We attended the trial every day, not out of a sense of duty, but because of our love for Cara."

Cara's father, Samuel Knott, read a prepared statement where he expressed his hope "that this predator will never walk the streets again."

"He kidnapped and murdered our sweet Cara, hiding behind his badge and breaking his sacred trust to society ... We want to make sure this terrible horror does not happen to someone else," he said. "Cara was innocent and she was special."

The case made a significant impact on many who followed it – particularly because of Peyer's previous reputation within the community, and the idea that a trusted member of society could commit such a terrible crime.

"I have been in this business for 44 years, and I have never seen a case affect a community like the Craig Peyer case," said Pfingst. "The only thing that was comparable was Son of Sam, back in New York."

Eventually, Peyer received a sentence of 25 years to life – but he's still never admitted to killing Cara Knott.

It was the second time Superior Court Judge Richard Huffman had presided over an emotional trial for Peyer, and he seemed to have a difficult time remaining composed as he imposed Peyer's sentence. Although he praised the efforts of the California Highway Patrol to restore public faith in the agency after Peyer had been arrested for Knott's murder, he admonished the officials also had to share some of the blame in her death.

He specifically pointed to an incident just one month before Knott was murdered on the dark, private Mercy Road off-ramp, when a mother had called the department with a complaint that Peter had forced her daughter to pull over along the same isolated road. The sergeant who took the complaint failed to take any decisive action to address the incident, Huffman said – "following the bureaucratic pattern of dismissing complaints."

He said officials with the highway patrol let Peyer "continue taking young women to the off-ramp, even after receiving complaints" – and added that the specific sergeant in question had gone so far as to "[commend] Peyer for his tactics."

"The tactics were wrong ... and they led inexorably to this tragedy, sure as the sun came up this morning," Huffman said. He added that if the agency had taken action based on the complaint from this concerned mother instead of dismissing the report, "Cara Knott would be alive and Craig Peyer would not be on his way to state prison."

When he refused a request from the defense to consider the possibility of probation for Peyer, Huffman's voice cracked and he seemed to be holding back tears. According to the judge, he'd received more than 100 letters and petitions on Peyer's behalf, from supporters urging Huffman to be lenient on Peyer, as it was his first offense.

Huffman refused.

"The crime, in this came, was an egregious, brutal crime ... The defendant took advantage of a position of trust and confidence ... He placed himself in a circumstance where he found it necessary to take the life of another person," he said. "... A young woman was brutally murdered on the very threshold of life ... I can't fix anything. All I can do is punish ... There's nothing I can do. One family has almost been destroyed by this, and the sentence that the court will impose will do the same thing to another. There's nothing I can fix."

The Golden Rule

After his daughter's death, Sam Knott put in countless hours establishing the Cara Knott Memorial Oak Garden near where Knott's body was found, in the Los Peñasquitos Canyon Preserve. The garden remains to this day, but is now the San Diego Crime Victims Oak Garden.

Right by the very spot where his daughter took her last breath, Sam Knott passed away in 2000 after suffering a heart attack when leaving the garden.

"I think about Sam a lot," admitted Pfingst. "Sam never recovered from that day ... and, ultimately, it killed him, right where his little girl died."

Peyer was contacted in 2004 by authorities from the District Attorney's Office. They offered to run DNA testing on key evidence as part of a wrongful conviction project, but Peyer declined. He was denied parole shortly after – the board concluded that Peyer continued to show a lack of remorse for the murder, and that although he continued to claim his innocence, he refused to allow anyone to try and prove it.

In 2007, he divorced from his third wife, Karen – whom he'd married just 18 months before Cara Knott's murder. Karen had visited him frequently prior to the termination of the marriage, and had defended her husband's innocence when he was initially convicted and sentenced. As she read the court a prepared four-page statement, she brushed tears off her cheeks. Her statement included references to love, compassion, and religion, and included condolences to the family of Cara Knott, who were seated on the opposite side of the packed courtroom.

"Cara Knott was a gorgeous, vivacious, well-loved young lady. During the trial, I felt the pain her family has had to endure, and I am deeply sorry that she was killed," Karen said. "But my husband was a friendly, vibrant, and well-loved person, too, and in my heart, I know you have the wrong man."

Until that point, Peyer hadn't shown any emotion in the courtroom – he'd even declined the opportunity to testify at this trials, and hadn't provided any public statements about the case at all. But as his wife spoke, he finally broke down in tears.

"From the time of Craig's arrest, he and our entire family have cooperated fully with everyone concerned, with the idea in mind of treating others how you would like to be treated," Karen said. "Unfortunately, that is not how the world is run; that is not how our legal system is run."

In addition to her bitter words about the legal system, Karen Peyer also expressed disgust with the way the media handled the case. An appeal had been denied to allow defense attorneys to question a reporter from the San Diego Union about documents which had apparently been leaked to the press, including the results of a polygraph test that had been given to Peyer prior to his arrest.

According to Huffman, the California Shield Law protected the reporter from having to provide information about his sources to the court, which frustrated Peyer's attorneys – and his wife.

"Before Craig's arraignment, the media had him tried and convicted," she stated. "By most people's expectations, the first trial was supposed to be a slam-dunk, and, when it wasn't, people began questioning, doubting, wondering. By the start of the second trial, we really believed there could be a fair and impartial trial held here in San Diego."

However, Karen claimed, "rumors" began circulating that things "were not going as planned," and a "tiny little tidbit" was forwarded to the local newspapers.

"A confidential, inadmissible piece of information, a lie detector test ... and now, the media pleads the Shield Act and screams it violates their rights," Karen said. "But it was all right for them to violate Craig's rights to a fair trial and to be above the law."

Her statement concluded with an expression of love toward her husband.

"I love you Craig, and I am glad to be your wife," she said. "I will always be committed to you."

Peyer's elderly parents also visited him in prison regularly, every other month, but both passed away in 2010.

A second parole request in 2008 was denied, and a third bid was rejected in 2012. At that time, the board ruled that Peyer wouldn't be eligible again for another 15 years – the longest time permitted under California state law. In 2027, when Peyer will once again be up for parole, he will be 77 years old.

Each time, Joyce Knott traveled to the prison to plead her case – to persuade the board not to grant parole to this man she now refers to as "the monster."

"I dread it. It's a dreadful thing to have to do," she said. "It's kind of beyond anything you can imagine, to go up and go into prison and go through those doors, and to be taken to this room and then the monster comes in."

The board of parole hearings also reads submitted letters, and Joyce always fiercely encouraged the public to send in a letter on her daughter's behalf, requesting that Peyer continue to be held behind bars. Obviously, her advocacy paid off.

Now in his late 60s, Peyer is serving his time at the California Men's Colony, a state prison located in San Luis Obispo. In 2008, at his second parole hearing, he told the board he had a "nearly unblemished prison record," and that he had "worked as an electrician at the facility" for several years – earning himself a salary of $52 per month in 2003.

"She's always with us."

Cara Knott would be in her 50s – and her mother, Joyce, said she still thinks about her daughter every day.

The third of Joyce and Sam's four children, Knott was "tender-hearted," Joyce recalled. An artist, an animal lover, and someone who "always had time for everybody."

"Her big thing was to be a mother and she really wanted to have children," Joyce said. "I have four grandchildren. I should have more, but I won't."

For more than a decade, Joyce was unable to touch the room her daughter had left vacant. But about fifteen years ago, it was time to put away some of Knott's old things and redo the empty bedroom – "which takes some courage," she admitted. When she pulled off the old wallpaper, though, Joyce uncovered a heartwarming surprise: carefully drawn flowers, with handwritten words left by her daughter – "My name is Cara Evelyn Knott. I am 14 years old."

"I appreciate the fact that people remember (her)," Joyce said. "She's always with us."

Knott's murder has had a lasting impact, however – in addition to inspiring several books and episodes of television shows like Forensic

Files and Investigation Discovery's Unusual Suspects, the case led to a change in state legislation.

Following the crime and the subsequent trial, many solo female drivers began refusing to pull over when ordered to do so by police officers or highway patrol. In response, the State of California issued a new mandate, allowing that drivers traveling alone would be able to proceed to a high-profile area if ordered to stop – a location like a mall or a gas station, with an increased likelihood of witnesses.

SHEILA LABARRE

15

ABBY MILLER

PROLOGUE

The farmhouse and surrounding area looked like something from the set of "Little House on the Prairie."

The house on Harvey Farm stood nestled in between tall pine trees, peaceful streams, and wildlife.

A place where you don't expect to find scenes that would be given an "X" rating if it were a horror movie.

The police arrived at the home while conducting a search for a missing young man named Kenneth Countje. They did not have to search far to find evidence of criminal activity. In the front of the property, lay a mattress burning alongside a smoking garbage barrel.

Their first inclination was to believe that the resident was burning garbage. A citation was due, maybe, but they had more pressing matters to attend to.

But upon closer inspection of the barrel, the officers saw a bone sticking out of the garbage.

A femur?

A mass of fleshy goo remained at the knob of the bone and the smell of the charred remains made the policemen gag.

They both gave each other a look of horror. Here in a town where the most serious crime would be a speeding ticket or jaywalking, the police were about to enter a whole world of horror beyond their wildest imagination.

CHAPTER ONE

Epping, New Hampshire.

Population = less than six thousand.

Epping is a rainy, small town that has been sarcastically nicknamed "The Center of the Universe". That has not stopped the residents from hosting parades, canoe races and music festivals. But when Sheila LaBarre arrived, the tiny hamlet soon became known for murder.

"She was a smart woman," forensic psychologist Paula Orange said. "Not book smart but intuitive. She could read people."

Sheila was born Sheila Kaye Bailey in Fort Payne, Alabama in 1958.

She was the youngest of six children. Her first marriage with a man named Ronnie Jennings would last less than two months. Jennings would find out that Sheila had been locking his child from a previous marriage in a closet to punish her. Jennings would divorce Sheila but she would find herself a new man in short order, tying the knot with John Baxter and moving to Chattanooga, Tennessee. Even though married, she would secretly fantasize about being swept away by a rich man. Sheila's mental illness would come to bear in her second marriage and that would end in divorce as well. Despondent, Sheila tried to kill herself and was sent to a psychiatric facility. She would be raped by an orderly inside the hospital.

Now single in Tennessee, the cash-strapped Sheila was forced to live in a local YMCA. She attended a church service and had a private talk with one of the preachers as she wanted "spiritual guidance." She would later claim that the reverend asked if she wanted to "sit in his lap." She then went to a psychiatrist who asked her if she had anal sex with any of her former husbands. The doctor then called Sheila at home and asked if "what she was wearing" and if she "was touching herself."

"If what we are to believe all of Sheila's stories," Orange said. "Then literally all of her interactions with men have ended with them as the pervert and her as the victim. Her sister would later testify that Sheila was molested by her father when she was young. Then her abusive marriages, the rape at the psych facility segues into a spiritual search where she meets a preacher who shows her the tent in his pants. Crazy."

CHAPTER TWO

Sheila turned to personal ads after her failures in marriage. She didn't like the normal courtship process of going to bars and meeting men there. She used the personal ads to cherry pick the men she wanted, men she could dominate.

"Whether on-line or off-line, Sheila behaved like a woman who was in complete control," Orange said. "She would develop a strange kind of power over men. It was almost as if she knew which men would be vulnerable to her feminine wiles and which ones would fight back. But when it came to Dr. Bill LaBarre, it was more of a case of getting the money."

While in Tennessee, Dr. LaBarre decided to take out a personal ad. He would get a response from Sheila who immediately sought to separate herself from the other paramours of the rich doctor.

She sent the doctor nude Polaroids of herself.

The strategy worked.

"She showed no shame in flirting with the older man and soon had him in the palm of her hand," Orange said. "He'd buy her fancy clothes, necklaces, the whole nine yards."

Wilfred "Bill" LaBarre was a successful chiropractor but lonely. Overweight and bespectacled, he had little to offer aside from his wealth. He was in his sixties and recently widowed.

Dr. Labarre was considered a good man by all who knew him. He had been the "Chiropractor of the Year" in 1983 but that would be the same year his beloved Edwina would pass away from cancer. Eager to salve the loneliness, he married another woman named Leona but she abandoned the doctor after a few years. He had two children from his first marriage; Laura and Gregory.

Now alone and widowed, the doctor wanted to spend his golden years enjoying his wealth.

And a young woman.

He would look at the nude Polaroids of the curvaceous Southern Belle, becoming obsessed.

"Here was a lonely, older man who all of a sudden had a 27-year old woman sending him nude photos. He thought he hit the jackpot."

Dr. LaBarre soon invited Sheila to come live with him at his farm in Epping, New Hampshire. The farm was a spacious one, a 115-acre horse ranch that according to LaBarre, "needed a female hand."

Sheila would become enamored by life on the farm, at least at first. She "never heard a June bug before" and the isolated country home gave her a peace that she never experienced.

Neighbors were not shocked that Dr. LaBarre took in such a younger woman as his girlfriend. He reportedly had other girlfriends after his wife died. "Sheila ran all the other girls off," one neighbor said.

But Sheila would prove to be a high-maintenance girlfriend. She would drain Dr. LaBarre's finances, making him buy her gifts and prizes which included a brand-new Silver Mercedes.

She also began to interject herself into LaBarre's estate and business dealings.

The farm that LaBarre owned was called the Old Harvey Farm. It was named after the original owners of the property who still lived in the area. But Sheila forced the doctor to change the name, she wanted it called something that reflected her personality.

The Silver Leopard Farm.

Sheila then had a sign made up and had it placed at the entrance.

She was marking her territory.

CHAPTER THREE

Despite the constant gifts and financial prizes, Sylvia proved to be an ungrateful sugar baby. The relationship would turn tempestuous after a few months. Sheila would claim that Dr. LaBarre often referred to himself as an "old fart" and looked the other way when Sheila began to have different men over for sex.

"He just worried about me when I would date far from home. But he was getting old and his heart would stop beating sometimes."

But the couple fought and police were routinely called to the residence to mediate their domestic disputes.

"You would sometimes hear gunshots," Bruce Allen, a LaBarre neighbor said. "You would hear her screaming, 'I'm going to kill you, you mother fucker!'"

Sheila once pulled a gun on the doctor and forced him out of the home. The chiropractor hid behind a boulder as his girlfriend shot at him.

LaBarre's daughter also recalled that she heard Sheila screaming threats at her father. "I'm gonna kill the horses and I'm going to kill you too."

Laura would later remark at how much her father changed after Sheila came into his life. He went from a normal, well-liked member of the community to a meek, submissive man.

"Sheila was all about being an opportunist," Orange said. "She had the ability to read a man, analyzing his weaknesses, size him up and then push the buttons. With LaBarre, she had a lonely man in front of her. He would tolerate anything in order not to lose her at first and then he simply became fearful of his life. These men in this small New England town did not have the wherewithal to deal with a violent sociopath like Sheila."

Sheila didn't stop with the renaming of Old Harvey Home. She soon took over the accounting duties at LaBarre's chiropractic business. She began organizing the practice into a well-oiled machine. She would track down patients who owed the doctor money and file numerous small claims in the Hampton District Court.

Concerned friends would advise him to dump Sheila before it was too late but it became apparent that the doctor either didn't know how or was afraid to. Dr. LaBarre informed neighbor Bruce Allen that he "had to get rid of her" and that he wanted to "send her back to Alabama. Hopefully, she'll stay there."

Her power over Dr. LaBarre increased to the point where he had given her power of attorney. She began rewriting his will, becoming the executor of his estate. The will stated that he was leaving everything to "a very special lady known as Sheila Kaye Jennings LaBarre."

"The will was very carefully redacted from the original," Orange said. "She kept a lot of the parts of the original and used her own typewriter to amend the little detail of where all the assets will go to. She was very astute and covered her tracks very well for someone who was supposedly schizophrenic."

The two would live together (Sheila would move out briefly but claim to be his common-law wife) from 1987 until LaBarre's death in 2000 at the age of 74. The coroner logged his cause of death as heart disease. There were suspicions among those close to the doctor that believe Sheila poisoned him to hasten the process.

"He was pretty old," Orange said. "And according to the autopsy, the heart disease was significant. So Sheila didn't have anything to do with his death despite the suspicions. The killings would come later."

Sheila would inherit the farm, LaBarre's Chiropractor office, two apartments and a rental home.

This was all valued at over two million dollars in assets.

Strangely, Sheila would marry a Jamaican national named Wayne Ennis in August of 1995 while living with Dr. LaBarre. Ennis drove a tour bus around Jamaica and Sheila made sure that when she toured the islands with Dr. LaBarre that they would cross paths with her Jamaican lover. She arranged for Ennis to obtain a visa and took him back to the farm with her. She would later claim that she and the doctor had stopped having sex and that she "had needs" which apparently Ennis took care of. She would later concede to pleasing the doctor sexually, "I'd use my hand," she said afterward.

Ennis would live in the farmhouse for almost a year. He had his own numerous encounters with Sheila which were violent and bizarre. One night, she ordered him to get in the car. The two then drove around the quiet town, Sheila's voice taking on a conspiratorial tone.

"I wish one of those damn horses would just kick him (Dr. LaBarre) in the head," Sheila said. "Kick him in the head and kill his old ass. I've thought about strangling him myself. But now I have a better idea. I want you to kill him."

Ennis was too frightened to say no to Sheila. The two would eventually divorce and the court records reveal that Sheila took out a restraining order against him.

Ennis disputed the allegations and stated that Sheila was the abuser.

He would later recall being punched, pushed, and shot at by Sheila.

"She told me that she was going to send me back to Jamaica in a box," Ennis said.

Dr. LaBarre told Ennis that Sheila was crazy and believed that she would eventually kill him. He gave the Jamaican money and sent him to the bus station, requesting that he leave town for his own safety.

After the relationship with Ennis ended, Sheila began dating James Brackett.

She and James would remain together for six years despite the fact that Sheila would attack Brackett with a pair of scissors, a machete, and an ax. When all of that failed she tried to shoot him.

The two would break up after which Brackett would get himself a vanity license plate that read "I'm Alive."

Brackett recalled moments where Sheila would act sweet and nice only to go into a violent rage moments later. He said that the greatest example was a time when he was taking a long bath with Sheila only to have her get out of the tub and smash him in the face with a two-foot grill brush.

Two of his teeth would be knocked out from the impact.

Sheila would attack Brackett for a variety of transgressions that would not be guilty of. Hurting her rabbits, damaging her property or having affairs with other women.

Brackett finally had enough, escaping from the farm on one rainy night and hitchhiking back into town.

"I'm lucky to be alive," he would later state.

CHAPTER FOUR

Sheila inherited the farm after LaBarre's death. The doctor's children tried to contest the will but were told that the odds of winning the case were 50/50 at best. They would also have to front over $50,000 to pay for the court costs.

Sheila soon turned the farm into her own private fiefdom. She would hire young men to help her around the place then pay them with her sexual favors or sometimes just beat the shit out of them.

"There would neighbors that would claim to see young men leave her house," Orange said. "They would look beaten up; black eyes, bloody lips, facial contusions. God knows what else."

Her neighbors began to suspect something fishy was going on but had no real evidence to call the police with.

"The first time I met Sheila LaBarre was at the Harvey Farm Stand," said Bonnie Meroth, one of Sheila's neighbors. "It was during the summertime when the produce was ready. I had no basic interaction with her except that of someone standing next to another person as a consumer. And she suddenly turned around and said 'I'll kill you if you come down to my farm' or words to that effect."

Bonnie would later claim that Sheila would try to scare her while driving down the road, nearly running her over while she was on her morning walk.

When she wasn't intimidating neighbors and townsfolk, Sheila would use the farm as the playground for her own private fetishes.

She liked to control and bully men. Stroking one of her pet rabbits, she would punish and insult the men unlucky enough to work at her farm.

"Are you kidding me?" Sheila yelled at the young man who dropped the wheelbarrow. "This should have been done yesterday."

He was young and naive, needing money. If it meant taking lip from Sheila, so be it. He needed work and she seemed nice when she hired him.

"Hurry up!" Sheila said, kicking the man in his buttocks. "Move, move. Are you kidding me? I've never seen a lazier man in my life."

Fatigued after working sixteen hours for seven days straight, the young man keeled over in exhaustion, dropping the wheelbarrow.

"Bitch made, perverted ass pedophile!" Sheila said. "Is this what I am paying you for? I am paying you to work. Now get off your bitch ass. Now!"

It became apparent that Sheila had a gift. A gift of controlling a certain type of man. Verbally abusive and overbearing, she encountered very little resistance.

She kicked the young man again. "Your name is 'bitch', you hear me?"

His real name was Michael Deloge.

CHAPTER FIVE

Deloge had problems as a teen. He got caught up in drugs and found himself on the streets, living out of homeless shelters. In 2004, he would meet Sheila LaBarre.

Deloge became smitten with the woman whom he saw as the life of the party. She would drink beer and play country songs on a guitar. According to Deloge's stepfather, Gordon Boston, the duo would indulge in drugs and study "sadistic material".

Deloge would join Sheila at her farm and soon become her personal whipping boy. Sheila would slap him around like a rag doll. One of the fellow ranch hands, Philip Sullos, recalled witnessing Sheila beating on Deloge with a hardwood stick until he bled. Deloge cowered and took the beating. She would then throw Deloge into a windowless shack and slam the door shut.

Deloge would cower meekly in the corner until Sheila came and got him, making no attempt to escape.

He would be declared missing in 2004 and no one would ever see him again.

In February of 2006, Sheila began looking for a new farmhand. She had her own criteria. He had to be young but pliable to her controlling methods.

She would find the perfect foil in Kenny Countie.

"Kenny was a lovely boy," Carolynn Lodge, Kenny's mother said. "He couldn't do enough for you. Everyone was his friend. I was so proud of him. He never had a horrible word for anybody and that was the problem. He trusted everybody."

Kenny's trust would lead him into Sheila LaBarre's trap.

Kenny would answer one of Sheila's personal ads. The young man was still naive and according to some reports had a "low IQ". The two met through a telephone personal ad service with Sheila calling up the young man and charming him in a way that no woman ever did.

"He (Kenny) told my son Brian that he met a 47-year old woman in New Hampshire," Lodge said. "She owned a farm. She owned a beautiful car. And she was rich. And he was serious about her."

"Kenny fit Sheila's psychological criteria," Orange said. "She targeted men whom she could overpower not only physically but also mentally. She was older than Kenny and light years more cunning. She knows exactly what to say and do to push his buttons. She takes the lead, telling him that he is going to be 'in for the time of his life' and that she 'can't wait to see him.' To a young man with limited experience and intelligence like Kenny, this is music to his ears."

Sheila would arrive at Kenny's home in the silver Mercedes. The silver leopard, the cougar, picking up her prey and taking him back to her lair.

Kenny's family would never see him again.

Sheila would use the same methods on Kenny as she did on the men in the past. She seduced the young man first then isolated him in her farmhouse. Then she berated him verbally before beating the shit out of him with face slaps, punches, and a wooden stick.

The beatings would come to a head during a weekend in February of 2000. Sheila beat Kenny's face into a pulp, took the wooden cane to his legs and may have poisoned him.

Then she decided to take him shopping at Walmart.

Placing him in a wheelchair, she rolled him around the outlet as she stocked up on garden supplies. She dumped two containers of diesel fuel into the prone Kenny's lap.

Little did he know that she would later use the gas to incinerate his body.

Customers gawked at the odd couple, concerned about the contusions on Kenny's face.

"Fuck you looking at?" Sheila would scream as she sped down through the aisle.

Employees of the store soon became concerned, calling the police.

The cops would arrive, confronting the couple in the store. They inquired about Kenny's condition but he didn't respond. Instead, Sheila took the lead, telling Kenny that he "didn't have to talk to these assholes."

The police didn't follow through. Kenny remained silent as Sheila rolled him through the store and out the door. No crime had been witnessed and they let the couple go.

Kenny's mother would later sue the police for negligence but it was tossed out of court in 2010.

A few nights after the Walmart incident, Sheila would make a frantic phone call to the police.

"I got a pervert in my house!" she screamed into the phone. "He's a pedophile! A pedophile!"

In a bizarre sequence of events, Sheila began to play a recording for the detective on the other end. She had routinely audio recorded everything she did, trying to incriminate the young men she worked with into admitting they were pedophiles. On this occasion, she played back a recording of her and Kenny.

"On the tape was my son, vomiting," Lodge said. "He kept saying 'he's faking, he's faking.'"

Sheila would ask Kenny if he was a pedophile on the tape. Kenny would answer 'yes'.

"Now he's a pedophile," Kenny's mother said. "Now he's raping children. Raping his brother. He's vomiting."

The police would write off the call as the rantings of a schizophrenic. They did not immediately respond to the residence.

Sheila would then kill Kenny Countie.

"She had to justify the killing of the young men in her own mind," Orange said. "For some bizarre reason, she would brainwash herself into thinking that her victims were pedophiles. She would repeat the question like a mantra, 'Are you a pedophile? Are you a pedophile?' Working herself up into an angry and violent state of mind before she killed the man."

Sheila's sister, Lynn Noojin, believed that Sheila was sexually abused by her father. Because of this, she became obsessed with child molestation. She would accuse the young men that worked for her of various sexual deviations, including pedophilia, incest, and bestiality.

CHAPTER SIX

After the bizarre call to police, authorities would not arrive at the farmhouse until the next morning. The police would enter the grounds, seeing both the burning mattress and barrel with Kenny's remains. They would not identify the burning bones as belonging to Kenny until much later.

Sheila had murdered Kenny the night before. She attacked Kenny ferociously with a kitchen knife, pushing the already weakened young man to the floor and stabbing away.

Blood sprayed and splattered everywhere.

Sheila then dragged Kenny's body out to her yard where she doused his body with the diesel fuel they had purchased at Walmart.

Lighting a match, she set the dead man on fire. She then took her pet rabbit in her lap, pulled up a chair and watched Kenny Countie burn.

"He was dismembered," Kenny's mother said, fighting tears. "And he was put in a pit and burned. But my son, he just wanted to be loved. I can't imagine what he must have been thinking. Because he was all alone."

Police would look throughout the house and find blood splatter on the walls and floor. A forensic team arrived and matched the blood with Kenny's DNA sample from his Army days. They would find the wallet of Michael Deloge but not his body.

Hundreds of police would spend seventeen days searching the 115-acre property. They found numerous burn pits and blood remains that were so old they had layers of dust on them. They would find clothing that belonged to Deloge and some toes that remain unidentified (it is rumored that the toes may belong to a mysterious Irish man who Sheila claims was stalking her.)

Going on the run from the cops, Sheila hitchhiked along Interstate 293. She was then picked up by Stephen Martello.

"Thanks so much for stopping," Sheila said.

"No problem," Martello said, looking the buxom Southern Belle up and down. His heart began to race.

Will he get lucky?

"My car broke down about two miles back. I got into a fight with my boyfriend and I'm trying to get to Dorchester."

"I'm headed that way," Martello said.

Sheila clutched her purse as if it were a security blanket and she kept looking back at the rear window.

"You all right?" he asked.

"Yeah," Sheila said "Just a little rattled. You know, it has been a tough day."

Martello took Sheila to the drug store when she said she needed to stop off and "buy some things". He tailed Sheila around the store until she bought a douche. Noting her erratic behavior, Martello disappeared out of Sheila's earshot to call the police on his cell phone.

"Hi," Martello said. "Just curious if you folks are looking for someone who just robbed a bank or an escaped mental patient. I just met a woman who is acting kind of strange."

When the authorities informed him that they were not actively investigating someone with that kind of background, Martello took Sheila to a hotel room.

The two would engage in wild and loud sex.

"You just had sex with an angel," Sheila proclaimed after they were done.

"Is that right?"

"You're not like the other men," Sheila said. "My boyfriend, Jesus, I just caught him with a huge stack of child porn. He is a pedophile. So are all those damn cops. Pedophiles, all of them. I think all sex offenders must die."

Martello said nothing. Instead, he put his pants and shoes on as fast as he could as Sheila continued to go on another bizarre rant.

"Vengeance is mine saith the Lord," Sheila said, laying on the bed in post-coital repose. "I was sent back to earth as an angel. I know how to speak to God in Hebrew. Do it every night."

Martello excused himself and high-tailed it out of the hotel room. He arrived home and saw the television broadcast about Sheila. He didn't call the police, worried that he would be an accessory to her crimes. Instead, Martello drove to the station and practically sprinted to the front desk.

"I think I just met Sheila LaBarre."

"To the end, Sheila had control over just about every man put in front of her," Orange said. "Here was a guy who picks her up at the side of the road. He thinks she is crazy enough to where he calls the cops to find out if there are any missing mental patients. He knows that she has a screw loose but he has sex with her anyway. It may be a poor reflection on men for sure but his response is typical. The men that Sheila encountered, from Dr. LaBarre all the way to Stephen Martello, all had the same false narratives going on in their head. They did not see a beautiful woman as something evil. It just didn't fit their narrative. So when Sheila begins her abuse, they just can't believe it. They refuse to hit a 'woman' back. She gets them 'pussy whipped' then beats the shit out of them. Rinse and repeat."

Sheila LaBarre would later be arrested for the murders of Michael Deloge and Kenneth Countje. She would plead no guilty on the grounds of insanity.

"This is a sick, sick woman," her attorney would argue. "Deeply disturbed."

Court-appointed psychiatrists would agree, testifying that Sheila was delusional as well as schizophrenic.

The jury would visit both LaBarre's farm and the Walmart where she frequented first hand. Sheila would join them as well although she was forced to wear a stun belt.

The jury did not buy her insanity defense and found her guilty.

"The fact that she has to remain for the rest of her life behind bars," Kenny's mother said. "She got what she asked for. She'll never see the light of day. Horrible thing is that my son, he's not here with me. He was only twenty-four."

Sheila LaBarre is now serving life in without possibility of parole.

INSTANT MESSAGE MURDERER: THE TRUE STORY OF SHAREE MILLER

MISSY COTTON

Chapter 1

Sharee Miller was a gorgeous, single mother-of-three when she met her husband Bruce Miller. At the time, she was in her early twenties, broke, and weeks away from being homeless.

The couple initially met when Sharee began working at Bruce's automobile scrap yard as a bookkeeper. After only three months, Sharee moved herself and her three kids into Bruce's house and they quickly became a family. Bruce gave Sharee a sense of stability she had never experienced and Sharee was kind, caring, and loving to Bruce.

After only a few more months, the couple married. Domestic bliss loomed on the horizon.

But six months later, Bruce was dead.

Initially, the events that led to Bruce's death were a complete mystery to police until a former homicide detective miles away shot himself in the head and left behind a briefcase of evidence.

How these two deaths were connected would shock police, and lead to one of the most infamous crimes in America.

Chapter 2

Sharee Miller, then Sharee Kitley, was born on October 13, 1971, in Flint, Michigan.

At the time, Flint was a powerhouse of economic growth largely due to the GM Buick and Chevrolet factories that operated in the city. General Motor's history was largely intertwined with Flint—the company's founder had formed the GM company in Flint in 1908. The GM factories in Flint were also the setting of the and iconic 1936-37 Sit-Down Strike—the strike that led to the creation of the United Auto Worker's union.

Flint made money because Flint made cars.

However, the Kitley family did not drink from the city's pool of wealth. They lived on the town's outskirts, a rough working-class neighborhood. They're home was a single-wide trailer smack-dab in the center of a tornado's playground. Sharee was an only child, she was the sole receiver of her parent's attention, but this attention was not desired by Sharee. Sharee's parents fought often, and when they were finished fighting with each other, they'd fight with Sharee.

In mid 80's, when Sharee was in her early teens, GM Motors closed its factories' doors in Flint. The city quickly fell to pieces, ramshackle remains of the auto empire it had once been. The city fell into a deep depression.

As she watched her hometown descend into ruins, Sharee decided to leave her toxic home for good. At the age of 16, Sharee moved in with her boyfriend at the time, and when that ended she couched surfed and work a variety of dead-end jobs, most of which only lasted a few months.

When she was 18, Sharee found herself pregnant and married to an abusive husband. The two shared a home in yet another low-income project in another rough neighborhood left in the dust of Flint's ruined automobile empire. Sharee watched her childhood repeat itself in front of her own eyes, but this time, it was her first-born son who held the starring role of the helpless child. Sharee ended the marriage after she caught her spouse physically abusing the young boy. It was one of the only lines Sharee drew in the sand—you did not harm her children.

Although Sharee took this brave step towards saving her son, history often repeated itself throughout her life. Two more failed attempts at finding a soulmate yielded two more children for the young woman. The single mother-of-three now resorted to frequently moving from low-income house to low-income house and took any odd job she could find—anything to keep her kids off the street.

Chapter 3

In 1997, Sharee was a single mother-of-three who was three breaths and an electricity bill away from being homeless. During an attempt to keep her kids safe and housed, Sharee took a job as a bookkeeper with B&D Auto, a small auto scrapyard that fit right in in the middle of Flint's automobile history.

Sharee had been hired despite having little-to-no experience keeping books in the past. She had convinced the boss, Bruce Miller, that she was hard-working, a fast learner, and desperate for a paycheque. And that seemed to be enough. That and the fact that Sharee was a stunner. Her bright blonde hair only drew more attention to her enrapturing icy blue eyes.

Bruce was a kind and generous soul. He took a chance on Sharee and it seemed to pay off. Only a few months after Sharee had begun working at the scrapyard, she and Bruce moved their relationship from the office to the bedroom. It wasn't long before Sharee and her three kids moved in with Bruce. The four now lived in a stable, secure home for the first time in any of their lives.

Bruce and Sharee married only months after they first met. Bruce, who has twenty-one his new bride's senior, thought he had finally found the perfect wife. Young, sexy, and loving. It was all he had ever wanted.

Her new life with Bruce was also a dream come true for Sharee. She had finally found a man that treated her right, and in him, she also found security. Ten years ago, she had left her own unhappy parents and embarked on a life of poverty and abuse. Now, she was sitting in the living room of a big house, watching her children—the true loves of her life—swimming in Bruce's above-ground pool. It was the idyllic life she never thought she could have.

But idyllicism did not suit Sharee.

Chapter 4

While Sharee lived the life she had always wanted for herself and her kids, Bruce's own family began to have doubts behind Sharee's motives.

Initially, Bruce's family took no issue with the fact that Bruce's wife was so young. The couple looked so happy and in love, they formed a perfect family. Bruce was even in the process of adopting Sharee's three boys. But things slowly began to change.

Sharee began to take advantage of her new wealth. She no longer worked at the scrapyard but began selling Mary Kay Cosmetics to other bored housewives instead. She began spending every penny of her earnings, and a whole lot more of Bruce's, on luxuries she had never been presented with before. She bought expensive jewelry and clothes, she got her first credit card plus a few more, and she bought an expensive computer for the home.

Bruce, however, did not partake in his family's worries. He was as happy as ever the day Jerry Cassaday stepped into his office and shot him square in the chest. Bruce understood Sharee's desire to buy things, he enjoyed watching her be careless with money for the first time in her life. And most of all, Bruce was proud that she began selling cosmetics door-to-door. An entrepreneur himself, he found Sharee's new profession to be ambitious. Bold. He had no qualms when Sharee brought home expensive dress after expensive dress, and he was nothing but proud when she showed him the computer she claimed was to help her keep track of all her sales.

If you had asked Bruce, he would have said the couple was as happy as could be.

Sharee, evidently, was not happy. Although she was pleased with the security her marriage to Bruce brought, she was bored. She was living the life of a housewife and simply got restless. She started going online and frequenting chat rooms where she could talk to strangers and meet new men. She could talk to these new men and Bruce would be none the wiser.

It was the perfect situation for Sharee. She got to keep the stable home life she knew she needed while engaging in the excitement of meeting new singles and falling in love without the latter threatening the first. In short, she got to have her cake and eat it too.

But this quickly fell apart. Soon, the satisfaction Sharee got from speaking to these men online began to fade. She needed more. She wanted to meet these men, feel their touch. This yearning was fresh in her mind the day she met Jerry Cassaday.

Chapter 5

Jerry Cassaday was working as a pit boss in a Reno casino. Before that, he had been a homicide detective and police officer for the Marshall Police Department and the Cass County Sheriff's Department. He began frequenting online chat rooms after his wife left him. He was lonely and had always wanted a family. He went online hoping to find companionship and an honest connection with a beautiful woman. Instead, he found Sharee Miller.

The two hit it off immediately. For Cassaday, it was love at first sight. He was enraptured by the blue-eyed blonde-haired twenty-something-year-old. There was only one problem: Sharee lived in Flint, Michigan and Cassaday was stuck in Reno, Nevada. They had no way to meet without arousing the suspicions of Sharee's husband Bruce until the perfect opportunity arose—a Mary Kay Cosmetics conference was announced. The location? None other than Reno, Nevada.

Sharee jumped at this opportunity to meet Cassaday in person and the spark they had struck up online burst into flames when they met in person. The two spent every free minute they had together, and Sharee even accompanied Cassaday to work. She would sit at his table and play hands of blackjack. When Cassaday finished for the night, the two would go back to Sharee's hotel room.

While Sharee was honest about being married at the time, she altered many details about her life in Flint to her favor. It was all part of the fantasy she had built up for herself online. Sharee told Cassaday that her husband was a high-ranking member of the mafia who frequently beat her and mistreated her children. They weren't in love, she was just too afraid to leave. Cassaday, who was in his mid 30's at the time, had always wanted a family and was aghast when Sharee told him the details about how her current husband treated herself and her kids. Little did he know it was all a lie.

The picture Sharee painted of her husband Bruce was so far away from the handsome, family-orientated business man that he really was. She wasn't describing reality, she was describing a fantasy. And Cassaday had bought it.

After Sharee inevitably left her new lover behind to return home to Flint, Sharee kept up their flame by sending numerous naked photos by email to Cassaday. They kept in constant touch through emails and instant messages. The two kept in touch so frequently that members of Bruce's family could later recall him complaining about the amount of time Sharee began to spend on her new computer. He knew something was up, he just wasn't sure what.

Sharee continued to build on the fantasy she had created with Cassaday. As well as nude photos, she would send him photos of herself covered in bruise-coloured makeup claiming they were from Bruce. On one special occasion, she went old school and snail-mailed Cassaday a tape labeled For Jerry's Eyes Only...

As Sharee fell deeper into the rabbit hole she had dug, two things became clear to her: the first, Cassaday was completely and utterly under her control, the second, she liked her new fantasy more than her real marriage.

Chapter 6

Sharee Miller's life had taken such a turn from her younger years. She had a stable life, a happy home, and a loving husband. But somehow, this was no longer enough for Sharee. Addicted to the danger of the unknown, Sharee had become bored in her easy marriage. She craved more.

She found the perfect path out of her marriage in Jerry Cassaday. Initially, the thrill of an affair was enough for her, but this eventually grew old—especially when her affair became online only.

Usually, when someone grows tired of their online relationship, they break up with their partner and cease communications. This was not the case with Sharee and Jerry Cassaday. When Sharee grew tired of her online affair with Cassaday she did not stop communications—she increased them. Although she had fallen out of love with the ex-homicide detective, she still needed him for one very specific purpose. He was going to kill her husband for her.

Cassaday had fallen madly in love with Sharee. He believed she was married to an abusive husband who has a high-ranking mafia player. He feared for his beautiful girlfriend and would do almost anything to protect her. Almost wasn't good enough for Sharee though. Sharee was going to use Cassaday to get out of her marriage, and to do so, she was going to have to make him mad first. Mad enough to kill.

Sharee's plan seemed foolproof. Bruce, her husband, was alone at his auto scrapyard a lot, and he always carried a large amount of cash on him, roughly $2000, in order to make change for his customers. Sharee saw this as the perfect opportunity. Someone could easily kill Bruce at his work with no witnesses, and better yet, if they took the cash on him, it would look like a robbery-gone-wrong. This would inevitably point police away from herself. All she needed was someone to pull the trigger.

Chapter 7

At some point during their online relationship, Sharee realized that she had Cassaday wrapped around her finger. She had seduced him in online and in-person and had maintained this enrapturement through sending him endless emails and seductive videos. Sharee began to use this power she had over Cassaday to make him angry. She had already painted her kind, gentle husband to be an abusive mafia man, but she needed more.

About a month after meeting with Cassaday in person, Sharee went to her local pharmacy and purchased a pregnancy test. She knew she wasn't pregnant—she had had her tubes tied after the birth of her third son—but she needed Cassaday to think she was. She went home, took photos of herself with her stomach pushed out, and sent them to Cassaday along with photos of the pregnancy test, which she had drawn lines on so it appeared to be a positive test. To make the lie seem more real, she also sent an image of her third child's sonograms.

I'm pregnant, she wrote Cassaday, with your first children. Twins.

A few weeks later, Sharee sent Cassaday more pictures of her stomach. This time, however, she coated her belly in blue and purple makeup first.

He killed our beautiful babies was the message sent along with the photos.

Cassaday was devastated, his lover's abusive husband had just taken from the world what he thought would be his opportunity to have a normal life with the woman he loved.

He fell into a severe state of depression. Cassaday could not take the news. He could no longer watch the woman he loved destroyed by her own oppressive husband. No. He was coming to town to free Sharee and finally have the family he'd always wanted.

Sharee was ecstatic. Through one later-debated series of instant messages, Sharee slowly revealed her perfect plan on how Cassaday should murder Bruce. The whole of Sharee's plan was summed up in only a few damning sentences.

I'll call Bruce at 5pm and tell him to call me when he's leaving. Pull up to the left side of the building, right to the door. He'll be at the desk inside. Take his wallet. Take the whole thing.

Chapter 8

On November 8, 1999, Jerry Cassaday drove from Reno to Flint to kill the man he thought killed his twin babies and repeatedly beat the love of his life.

He followed Sharee's instructions to the word. At 5pm he pulled up to Bruce Miller's auto scrapyard, went inside, shot Bruce in the chest, and took Bruce's wallet. Bruce was on the phone with Sharee at the time, just as she had planned. Sharee had chosen to listen to her husband die.

Cassaday's experience as a homicide detective meant that he could commit the crime without leaving forensic evidence behind. He left the scrapyard office without leaving a single finger or footprint and took Bruce's wallet without ripping the pocket, a general characteristic of a rushed robbery.

Investigators were also unable to recover any trace fibers or hairs from the scene or Bruce's body.

After committing the crime he had spent the majority of his life solving, Cassaday turned his car around and headed straight back to Nevada.

Chapter 9

A few hours after listening to her lover shoot her husband, Sharee called her brother-in-law Chuck Miller. She frantically told him that Bruce was missing, he hadn't come home for dinner and his work phone wasn't working. She convinced Chuck to drive out to the scrapyard to check on his brother.

When Chuck arrived, he was affronted with a horrible scene—Bruce was laying face down on the ground dead from a gunshot wound to his chest. His telephone receiver was on the ground next to his face. Within an hour, a full team of homicide investigators were on the scene.

Due to the lack of physical evidence at the scene, investigator's initially had little to go on. The main motive appeared to be robbery, just another day in Flint.

Sharee was brought in for questioning but was never suspected by police. She had been at home all day with her children and several friends. They simply wanted to ask her if she had any idea of who would want her husband dead, and Sharee was prepared for this.

Sharee told detectives that one of her former boyfriends John Hutchinson had owed Bruce several thousands of dollars. Bruce and Hutchinson had several arguments about this as well as the tumultuous state of Sharee and Hutchinson's former relationship.

Hutchison unluckily had no solid alibi. He quickly emerged as the key suspect in Bruce's murder.

To make things worse for Hutchinson, he had agreed to take a lie-detector test to prove his innocence, but the examination did not go smoothly. In the middle of the test Hutchinson collapsed and ended up going to the hospital. Not only had he failed the few questions he had been asked, but he was so clearly stressed about the test that he had physical symptoms.

The general feeling amongst investigators was that Hutchinson had killed Bruce, they just couldn't prove it. While his autopsy revealed that Bruce had been shot by a 20 gauge shotgun, Hutchinson did not own this type of gun and investigators failed to find one during a search of his home.

Eventually, much to Sharee's delight, the case went cold. It wasn't until a seemingly unrelated suicide miles away took place before police had any reason to suspect Sharee.

Chapter 10

After he returned to his home in Reno, Jerry Cassaday expected his relationship with Sharee Miller to continue as usual. He believed that they would continue to date long-distance until the murder investigation cooled down. Then, Sharee would begin a new life in Reno with Cassaday.

This, however, was not the case.

Sharee barely contacted Cassaday after the death of her husband. She didn't initiate any conversations and stopped replying to his emails altogether. Cassaday, still deep in the world of lies Sharee had created, began to panic.

A few weeks after killing her husband, Cassaday decided to pay Sharee a visit to make sure she was doing okay. When he arrived at her home in Flint, his world fell apart.

Sharee was at home with her three kids and a new boyfriend.

She had double-crossed Cassaday within weeks of the murder. Cassaday instantly returned to the state of depression he had been in when he believed that Bruce had killed his baby twins-to-be.

Sharee and Cassaday never spoke again, and Sharee had almost entirely forgot about her ex-lover when police started knocking on her door again.

Chapter 11

Seven hundred miles away from Sharee and Flint, in Kansas City, Missouri, Jerry Cassaday was found dead in his home, a gun in his hand, Bible in his lap, shot in the head. Cassaday could not live with the crimes he had committed for love, especially knowing that the love he felt wasn't real. It was too much for him.

Before he killed himself, Cassaday took measures to ensure his death would be connected back to Sharee and Bruce Miller's murder. Next to his body, police found his open briefcase which contained his suicide note addressed to his parents and a printed transcript of extensive instant messaging conversations. Outside in the trash, investigators also found a scandalous video of a young woman dancing naked addressed directly to Jerry.

Police showed clips of this video to Jerry's neighbors in order to identify the woman dancing. Several neighbors were able to identify Jerry's online girlfriend Sharee, who lived in Flint. When Kansas City police called the Flint sheriff's office to get more information about Sharee, Flint police were astounded. They instantly knew they had been duped by the blonde, beautiful widow.

When she was identified by Kansas City police, Sharee was immediately connected not only to Cassaday's suicide but also back to her ex-husband Bruce's murder. In his suicide note, Cassaday revealed that he had been the one to kill Bruce. Sadly, it was evident that he still believed many of the lies Sharee had told him. He stated in his note that he had to do it, Bruce had killed his children and that was something he couldn't let go. Even if it meant destroying his own life in the process.

He also described Sharee's role in the murder plot. He stated that she had encouraged him to commit the murder and helped him plan it. He could not have done it without her help. And he had provided investigators with the transcripts to prove it.

Sharee miller was brought in for questioning where she claimed she did not even know Jerry Cassaday. She stuck to this story until police revealed that they had the tape of her dancing, addressed in her handwriting as being For Jerry's

Eyes Only. After this, she was forced to change her story. It was undisputable evidence that they had had a relationship.

Sharee then told police she had met Jerry in a computer chatroom while just messing around, trying to figure out something new to do. Computer forensic experts then confiscated both Sharee and Cassaday's computers. What they found inside answered some important questions but raised many others.

Investigators easily found their way into Sharee and Cassaday's private online conversations. They found incriminating evidence on Jerry's computer—the online copy of the instant messaging conversation in which Cassaday and Sharee discussed Bruce's murder. When they confronted Sharee with these messages, she had a planned response: Cassaday was framing her.

Sharee told investigators that in the triangle of herself, her ex-husband Bruce, and Jerry Cassaday, Cassaday was the scorned lover. After she got bored with her online affair, she tried to cut contact with Cassaday, but he wouldn't let her. She claimed that Cassaday had forged the messages to implicate her in something she had never been apart of. Investigators thought that this claim was far-fetched, so they reached out to AOL, the company that hosted the instant messaging service Cassaday and Sharee used to communicate. Surprisingly, AOL took Sharee's side on the issue—it was possible for the messages to have been forged.

Investigators were now tasked with proving the legitimacy of the instant messages that showed Sharee had helped plan Bruce's murder with Cassaday. Under court order, AOL released information about Sharee and Jerry's computer activity. They confirmed that both Jerry and Sharee had been online and logged into the AOL service the same day at the same time for the same length of time as the instant message indicated. Police also found handwritten notes copied in Sharee's writing that listed information found in the messages. If they had been forged, Sharee would not have known this information in order to write it down.

Sharee was now trapped. Although she continued to maintain her innocence, investigators continued to find more and more damning evidence against Sharee.

Sharee had taken steps to cover her online footprints. A day and a half after the death of her husband she had called AOL to change her first name, last name, and her address. After she learned of the suicide of Jerry Cassaday, she did the same thing again. She was clearly worried about the content of her online messages being traced back to her.

Once investigators had confirmed the legitimacy of the messages, they were able to read the diary of Sharee's relationship with Cassaday. They were able to see how she was able to bring Cassaday to a boil, both sexually and emotionally. She brought him into her world the way she wanted him to see it.

Sharee had used her body, in so many ways, to intrigue, seduce, and trap the ex-homicide detective. The only thing that brought her down in the end was Cassaday's conscience on his dying day.

Further, Sharee's actions after her husband's death provided a possible motive for Bruce's murder other than Sharee's freedom. Money.

While Sharee had been loose with money during her marriage, she had gone over-the-top after her husband's death. She used Bruce's life insurance money to dramatically renovate her new inherited home within weeks of his death. She bought herself a new car and spent thousands of dollars on a plethora of items.

When Bruce died, Sharee inherited the family home she had grown so attached to as well as large sums of money both from Bruce's life insurance policy and also from the sale of his auto scrapyard business. Most significantly, though, Sharee had inherited her freedom without having to sacrifice her own and her children's secure, stable life.

Chapter 13

In December, 2000, Sharee went on trial for murder and conspiracy to commit murder.

Throughout the trial, Sharee continued to maintain that the instant messages were forged, as she was innocent of everything. She was simply the victim of an angry lover's broken heart.

The prosecutor's relied heavily on forensic science in their case against Sharee Miller—specifically, on the forensic computer analysis which proved the authenticity of Sharee and Cassaday's messages.

Sharee's trial was a short one. It did not take the prosecutors long to form their case, and the defense presented little-to-no evidence to support Sharee's claims that she was being framed by a dead man.

Sharee was found guilty on the charges of second-degree murder and conspiracy to commit first-degree murder. She was sentenced to life without the possibility of parole.

But this was not the end of Sharee's story.

Chapter 14

In 2009, Sharee Miller was released from prison after serving only nine years of a life without parole sentence. Her release was mandated by a U.S. District Judge who believed that the convicted killer had grounds for a new trial. This was because Jerry Cassaday's suicide note had been presented as damning evidence against Sharee in court despite the fact that Cassaday could not be cross-examined regarding the information in the letter.

Sharee spent a whole three years outside of bars. During this time, she kept a fairly low profile. She stayed in Flint with family, who she spent the most time with. She also spent the three years reconnecting with her sons—the children she spent most of her younger life fighting to support. Sharee's luck finally seemed to be turning in her favor.

But lady luck is fickle. In 2012, Sharee was ordered back to prison by the U.S. Supreme Court. The court disapproved of Sharee's release and mandated that the judge repeals her earlier decision to grant Sharee a new trial. The Supreme Court believed that there was enough additional evidence presented by the prosecutors, with no viable defense to counter it, that the outcome of the trial would have been the same had the suicide note not been presented at all.

Sharee's lawyers told the public that she was simply "disappointed" by her return to prison.

After returning to prison, Sharee and her lawyers quickly filed several appeals targeted at both the decision to return Sharee to court and her original guilty conviction, both of which were lost. Sharee was set to spend the rest of her life in prison for good this time.

That again seemed like the end of Sharee's story until late April 2016.

Seventeen years after manipulating Jerry Cassaday into killing her husband, Sharee Miller admitted her involvement in the crime for the first time through a letter addressed to a County Judge.

In this letter, Sharee claimed that she got caught up in the fantasy world she created with Cassaday. She like being the victim. It was more exciting to her than her real, stable life. However, she quickly found herself in too deep. She had created a monster and the only real way she saw of getting out was through the murder.

If Bruce were to die, neither he nor his family would ever have to discover what she was doing behind his back.

Sharee stated in her confessional letter that she did not enjoy watching her husband die. She wrote, "I had sixteen and a half hours to stop it. And I didn't. I knew it was going to happen and I allowed it. I allowed a man to kill another man based on my lies and manipulation."

She also used her letter as an opportunity to publicly recant the horrible image she had painted of her husband through her messages with Cassaday. She confirmed that Bruce was nothing but a wonderful husband. He had never laid a finger on her, and he always treated herself and her three children with the utmost kindness and respect. She regretted being the reason her children lost such a wonderful father figure—something she had always wanted for them.

While Sharee certainly believed that her confession would put an end to the long-standing controversy surrounding her case, the kind of controversy that inspired both a novel and lifetime movie about her crime, it actually perpetuated a new kind strand of controversy.

To many, especially to Bruce's loved ones, Sharee's confession letter seemed too crafted to be sincere. Sharee was the woman who had manipulated men to kill and die for her all through text. Now, she seemed to be trying to manipulate her way to an earlier release through the same medium.

Whether Sharee will claim another victim as a fool, this time a court judge, is yet to be seen.

A COUPLE WHO KILLED

Natalie Marshall

James Marlow and Cynthia Coffman were a troubled couple who were convicted of murdering five people during a deadly rampage that spanned multiple states. The last two victims, 20-year old Corrina Novis and 19-year old Lynell Murray were kidnapped and found strangled and sodomized, and the murderous pair were found guilty of the crimes. Whereas both Marlow and Coffman received the death penalty for Novis' death, Marlow received a second death sentence for Murray's while Coffman was sentence to life without the possibility of parole in Murray's murder. Both defendants sought to shift the onus of blame to the other with Marlow claiming it was Coffman's idea to kill the girls while he only wanted to rob them and Coffman alleging that she was the victim of battered women's syndrome. Neither ploy was successful as the pair were convicted across the board for robbery, kidnapping, sodomy, and murder. Coffman has the distinction of being the first woman sentenced to death in California following the state's reinstatement of the death penalty in 1977.

Early Lives

James

James Gregory Marlow was born on 11 May 1956 in Ohio but raised in Kentucky; the son of a beautiful but amoral hillbilly woman named Doris who virtually ensured that her son would grow up completely dysfunctional. Throughout his childhood, Marlow witnessed abuse, neglect, drug use, and sex courtesy of his mother who often prostituted herself in front of him. She gave birth to another child, Veronica Koppers, in 1959 and would frequently leave her children alone or with neighbors. Marlow eventually went to live with his father, Arnold, who would beat him severely and lock him in cabinets and, subsequently, went back to his mother's house. Despite the abuse and her horrific behavior, Marlow loved his mother dearly. So much, in fact, that when he was 13 years old his mother shot him up with drugs and seduced him. During interviews Marlow openly admitted to having had sexual relations with his mother on several occasions and that he didn't know it was wrong. He loved his mother so much and thought it was normal. Experts assert that Marlow suffered from traumatic bonding in which a traumatic event—his mother's seduction—created a dysfunctional yet significant bond from which he could not escape.

By the time Marlow was 16 years old he was living alone in California and married his first of three wives. Thanks to his mother, Marlow developed a severely skewed view of women. When she died in a trailer fire he was completely distraught and "took on the sins of his parents" by turning to a life of crime and violence. In one incident when he was still a teenager, Marlow was talking to one of his cousin's girlfriend, Darlene Miller, who he—one day while driving her to a nearby convenience store—pulled over in front of an old, abandoned house and forced Miller into the house where he beat and hogtied her, and then locked her in a closet. Over a span of three days Marlow would repeatedly beat, rape, and sodomize Miller. She escaped and ran to a neighbor's house—a house that Marlow had recently burglarized. Police were called and Marlow was arrested and after a tearful pretrial interview wherein he tearfully detailed the issues with his mother, he was sent to a drug rehabilitation center in 1975 for seven months and, soon after his release in 1976 was rearrested for being under the influence. Marlow was eventually imprisoned for burglary, robbery, and drug charges and was ultimately sentenced to California's notorious Folsom Prison in 1980. It was here that Marlow—not unlike the majority of inmates—got heavily tattooed with one—a howling wolf on his right side—earning him the nickname of the Folsom Wolf.

Prior to meeting Coffman, Marlow had an extensive criminal record. On 5 November 1979 in Upland, California, Marlow and his friend Allen Smallwood, who were both heroin addicts, assaulted Jeffrey Johnson in his apartment, searched it for non-existent drugs, then took Johnson downstairs—by knifepoint—to the Liesches' apartment where they searched the second apartment for more non-existent drugs, tied up the residents—Lori and Kathy—with electrical cords, and stole some cash they had found.

The following day, Marlow entered an Upland, California, leather goods store owned by Joanne Gilligan who was helping a customer, said he had a gun in his pocket and ordered them to lie on the floor, and then robbed the register of cash and took two jackets.

At approximately 10:00 a.m. on 20 November that same year, Gertrude Smith and Wilson Lee were working at an Ontario, California, methadone clinic when Marlow and Smallwood entered brandishing a sawed-off shotgun and pistol, respectively, and demanded methadone which they were told was locked in a safe. Another employee opened the safe and the two left with methadone that had a street value of $10,000. When Marlow was finally arrested on 26 November he had a bottle of methadone in his jacket and had the shotgun wrapped in a shirt.

Cynthia

Cynthia Lynn Haskins was born on 19 January 1962 in St. Louis, Missouri. From the beginning her life was to be difficult. Born with a double hernia that precluded her mother from holding her, Cynthia never experienced the necessary mother-infant bonding so crucial for healthy adjustment. As a result, she suffered from a crucial lack of empathy and a driving propensity to seek affections elsewhere. Cynthia's father left when she was three years old and her mother—who had aspirations of becoming a singer—allegedly tried to give her and her brothers Robbie and Jeff away several times during their childhood; with Jeff eventually given up for adoption. Cynthia was frequently "farmed out" to relatives that made her become more rebellious, defiant, and reckless. By the time she was a sophomore in high school, Cynthia was already experimenting with marijuana and methamphetamine with her new friends.

Her mother remarried a successful businessman named Bill Maender with whom Cynthia did not get along. Truancy, rebelliousness, and ultimately not wanting to live by her stepfather's rules caused Cynthia to run away at age 17 to her boyfriend's, Ron Coffman, house. When Cynthia returned three months later, pregnant, abortion was not an option for her devout parents and she refused to give the baby up for adoption, so she was forced into a loveless marriage with Coffman. The marriage quickly deteriorated and Ron filed for divorce because of Cynthia's infidelities, drug use, and poor housekeeping while Cynthia accused him of physical and emotional abuse and infidelity. Cynthia then worked in a carburetor factory to take care of her son, Joshua. She ultimately abandoned Joshua after two years, leaving him with her ex-husband (allegedly intending to get him back after she got settled) although later, when she and Marlow were committing their heinous crimes she suggested that Marlow kill her ex-husband and ex-in-laws (who had legal custody of Joshua) so she could regain custody of her son. While on death row Coffman exchanges letters with her son who believes his mother to be in prison for drug-related charges. She has stated in interviews that she wants to be the one to tell him the truth someday.

There is much speculation that Coffman had antisocial personality disorder which is characterized by little regard for right and wrong or the feelings of others. Further, those with the chronic disorder tend to manipulate, antagonize, and treat others with a callous indifference, are very prone to violate the law, are easily angered, lie, behave impulsively and/or violently, and use and abuse drugs and alcohol—all without remorse or guilt. Coffman exhibited a number of these traits, many of which worsened once she began her relationship with Marlow.

In May 1984 Coffman left home with a girlfriend and journeyed west where she wound up in Page, Arizona, and moved in with her new boyfriend, Doug Huntley. The lovebirds moved to Barstow, California where Huntley had some friends. He secured employment in construction while she was a bartender and waitress and sold methamphetamines on the side. One evening they were involved in an altercation outside of a convenience store in which Coffman pulled a gun on several men who were hassling her boyfriend and this resulted in both Huntley and Coffman being arrested and jailed. While Coffman was released after a few days, Huntley became cellmates with Marlow. Huntley told Marlow all about Coffman which intrigued Marlow who, upon his release soon thereafter, showed up at Coffman's apartment. It was love at first sight as Coffman reminded Marlow of his mother and Marlow was every bit the bad boy to whom Coffman was attracted. Even after Huntley was released, Marlow, Coffman, and he remained friends until Huntley returned to prison in June of that year.

A Dangerous Partnership

Marlow and Coffman began their contentious, dysfunctional, and murderous relationship amidst drugs and violence; her former boyfriend Huntley all but forgotten. In June 1986 Marlow had Coffman drive him to Fontana, California, and to his cousin Debbie Schwab's house where he purchased methamphetamines. A few days later they went to Newberry Springs and stayed with some of Marlow's friends, Steve and Karen Schmitt. Marlow told Coffman that he was a hit man, a martial arts expert, and a White supremacist who had murdered African American while in prison. It was during this time that Coffman saw Marlow turn into "Wolf"—his angry, violent alter-ego. Coffman testified in court that Marlow would beat her and then apologize and things would be fine again for a while. This is classic cycle-of-violence behavior central to most domestic violence cases. At this point Marlow allegedly took Coffman's address book that had her mother's and son's addresses and refused to give it back to her; essentially holding it as a carrot just out of reach to get her to do what he wanted.

They traveled across the country visiting Marlow's relatives in Kentucky and Tennessee. He had told Marlow that his father had recently died and left him some land in Kentucky and that they could get her son and live as a family there. First, however, they needed a vehicle and Marlow allegedly pressured Coffman to steal her friend's red Nissan pickup truck that Marlow and friend Paul Donner painted black. Marlow and Coffman jumped in the truck, stole some license plates from an off road vehicle outside of Newberry Springs, California, and headed east.

In Woodland Park, Colorado, Marlow called Gene Kelly, a contractor who constructed microwave telephone relay towers and who Marlow had met when he was a temporary laborer for him a few years back, to see if he needed any help in Colorado at the time. (There is some discrepancy in the available literature with respect to this individual being named Gene Kelly or Elmer Lutz; however, the actual criminal case against the defendants state Kelly). Kelly told him that he didn't have any work at the time but that he would have some work in Atlanta, Georgia, in a few weeks. The couple went to Colorado Springs for a couple of days and then to St. Louis to see Coffman's grandmother. They arrived on 2 July and Coffman called her mother who was less than happy to hear from her. The couple continued their journey east.

In Pine Knot, Kentucky, Marlow called his cousin Donald "Lardo" Lyons and both he and Coffman stayed with him for several days. Marlow had expected a modest inheritance from his grandmother Lena Walls with whom Marlow and his sister Veronica were close when they were younger; however, by the time Marlow reached Kentucky there was nothing left for him. Needing money, Marlow agreed to meet with Lardo's friend Shannon "Killer" Compton and the trio discussed how a local man named Greg "Wildman" Hill was going to be testifying in court against a mutual acquaintance and that Hill should "be silenced." They arranged for Compton to give Lyons a sum of money of which Lyons would give $5,000 to Marlow to get rid of Hill.

The next day, 7 July 1986, Lyons gave Marlow a .22 caliber pistol and at 5:00 a.m. Marlow and Coffman got into their stolen black Nissan pickup and drove to Hill's house. For most of the day the two of them parked relatively close and surveilled his house, did drugs, and engaged in sex. Finally, Marlow ordered Coffman to take off her shirt and bra and to tie a bandana across her chest like a bikini top and to knock on Hill's door to elicit help for her "stalled" truck. Hill agreed and tucked his own pistol inside his jeans' waistband. At the truck, when Marlow came after Hill with his own gun, Hill drew his and after an ensuing struggle Hill's gun went off, mortally wounding him with a bullet to the head. Marlow wiped his fingerprints off Hill's gun and left it at the scene.

Lyons kept true to his word giving Marlow the $5,000 "fee" for his "hit." The next day Marlow gave the stolen Nissan to a relative and spent $3,000 on a Harley Davidson; something he wanted for a very long time. On 11 July 1986 Marlow and Coffman had a "biker" wedding atop a Marlow's new Harley. Witnesses alleged that Coffman's face was bruised and scratched from a recent beating Marlow have given her. Such violence was not an isolated incident. In fact, one time while Marlow was assaulting Coffman one of his acquaintances asked what he was doing and Marlow dislocated his arm. As a result, nobody else ever intervened when Marlow was in one of his rages against Coffman. She said that when Marlow turns into "Wolf" his voice becomes monotone and his eyes and facial expression changes—that he becomes a completely different and violent person.

Marlow ended up giving the Nissan to a friend and purchasing a 1970's Cadillac to continue their journey to Atlanta and a job with Kelly. Marlow did manage to work for four days before an incident wherein he, Coffman, and a group of coworkers went out for dinner but which turned into Marlow beating Coffman outside of the restaurant and inside the vehicle, seemingly because she assisted some men with a stuck ball at a pool table. Back at the hotel where they were staying, Marlow was not finished with Coffman. He asked her for her scissors and then queried, "Your hair or your eye?" Horrified, Coffman said her hair and Marlow cut it as short as he could with her small scissors. He then taunted her that he would pierce her eye as well before making her strip naked and forcing her to stand outside the hotel room for several minutes. He then let her back into the room where he forcibly sodomized her. The following morning Marlow found a check from Kelly that had been slid under the door for his four days of work. After a few more days of going on "pot hunts" and unsuccessfully attempting a burglary in July 1986 in Whitley County, Kentucky, the couple left and headed back to Arizona.

In Arizona, Marlow and Coffman burglarized her former boyfriend Doug Huntley's parents' house and stole their safe that contained ten silver dollars—which they kept—and some papers. They buried the safe in the dessert. The next stop was back in Newberry Springs, California, where the couple stole two rings from the Schmitts; one they pawned for cash and the other they traded for methamphetamines.

Returning to Fontana, California, in early October 1986, Marlow and Coffman stayed with his cousins, the Schwabs. During their visit Marlow tattooed "Property of Folsom Wolf" on Coffman's buttocks and the word "W-O-L-F" and some lightning bolts on her ring finger as a wedding band. They then spent some time with Marlow's friends Rita Robbeloth and her son Curtis, and then with his sister, her husband Paul Koppers, and his brother, Steve. During this time Coffman alleges that after asking for an equal share of the methamphetamine they had, Marlow became angry and beat her, threatened to kill her, forced her to consume pills he said were cyanide, extinguished a cigarette on her face, and stabbed her in the leg. The pair then went to stay with another of Marlow's friends, Richard Drinkhouse.

The Crimes

On 11 October 1986 they were linked to the death of 32-year old Sandra Neary of Costa Mesa, California who never returned from a quick trip to a local ATM machine to withdraw some money. Her car was found in a nearby parking lot and her body was later found on 24 October by some hikers near Corona, California. Their next victim was 35-year old Pamela Simmons. She was reported missing in Bullhead City, Arizona, on 28 October. Her abandoned car was found by the local police department and the theory was that she was also abducted while withdrawing money from an ATM.

Corinna Novis

On 7 November, 20-year old Corinna Novis vanished from a First Interstate Bank parking lot near a shopping mall in Redlands, California, in broad daylight. Alone, she was driving her white Honda CR-X and when she failed to make her manicure appointment at her friend Terry Davis' salon, and then failed to make a 7:00 p.m. pizza date with other friends, she was reported missing. That same day, Marlow and Coffman were at the Redlands Mall visiting his sister Koppers who worked at a restaurant and were supposed to pick her up from work; however, Marlow gave his sister back her keys, telling her that they already had a ride. Coffman, clad in a dress, and Marlow, in a suit and tie, probably seemed rather innocuous to Novis when they asked her for a ride. Earlier that day Marlow had told Coffman that they needed to "get a girl" but Coffman alleged that she did not know that Marlow intended to kill her.

At approximately 7:30 p.m., they took Novis to Marlow's friend Richard Drinkhouse's house who was home alone recovering from a motorcycle accident at the time. Coffman took their hostage into the bedroom after telling Drinkhouse they needed to use the bathroom. Marlow told Drinkhouse that Coffman was trying to get her ATM pin number so they could "rob" her bank account. Drinkhouse didn't appreciate their intrusion into his house to which Marlow assured Drinkhouse that that there wouldn't be any witnesses because how could Novis talk to anyone "if she's under a pile of rocks"? Soon thereafter, Marlow's sister Koppers showed up and she and Coffman left the house to go to a nearby 7-Eleven while Marlow cautioned Drinkhouse not to leave and then returned to the bedroom where Novis was. After Coffman returned, she went into the bedroom to change clothes and after what sounded like the shower running the three of them emerged from the bedroom—Novis' and Marlow's hair were wet (Coffman testified that she had nothing to do with "what went on in the shower"). Novis was handcuffed and had duct tape over her mouth. They left the house and Drinkhouse testified that he never saw Novis again.

The next day, Marlow and Coffman asked Drinkhouse if he wanted to buy an answering machine. Novis' employer Jean Cramer, went to check on her the morning of 10 November when she uncharacteristically failed to appear at work and didn't call. She noticed Novis' car was missing, her front door was ajar, and her bedroom was in disarray. There was no evidence of forced entry and Novis' typewriter and answering machine were missing. On 7 November Koppers sold Novis' answering machine to a friend in exchange for a half-gram of methamphetamine who sold it to someone else and the Redlands Police Department ultimately recovered it. The next day, Harold Brigham who owned the Sierra Jewelry and Loan in Fontana testified that Coffman pawned Novis' typewriter using the victim's identification.

Back at the Robbeloths' house Coffman said Marlow changed clothes and tried to access money from Novis' account at a local First Interstate Bank; however, the PIN number she gave them was incorrect. The following day they ransacked Novis' apartment, found her PIN number, stole her money, pawned the typewriter they stole, disposed of Novis' belongings and then returned to Drinkhouse's house. On 12 November Marlow found out that his sister was in police custody and he and Coffman drove to Big Bear to get rid of Novis' car. They checked into the Bavarian Lodge using a credit card from another victim, Lynell Murray. They abandoned Novis' car on a dirt road south of Santa's Village which was approximately a quarter mile off of Highway 18 in the area. Coffman's fingerprints were found on the license plate, hood, and ashtray while Marlow's prints were found on the hood. The two then proceeded to walk along Big Bear Boulevard clad only in bathing suits despite the chilly weather; the stolen clothes that they had been wearing were discarded along with the handcuffs used on Novis. Receipts for clothing purchased by Marlow and Coffman were found in the clothing's pockets. The .22 caliber pistol the couple owned was in Coffman's purse.

Novis' body was discovered on 15 November lying face down in a shallow grave at a Fontana vineyard. She had been strangled and sodomized.

Dr. Gregory Reiber performed Novis' autopsy on 17 November and conclude that time of death was between five and ten days prior. Evidence of marks on her neck, injuries to her neck muscles, and thyroid cartilage fracture suggested death by strangulation; however, the presence of dirt in her throat also suggested possible suffocation. There was also biological evidence of sodomy.

Lynell Murray

On 12 November, 19-year old psychology student and Prime Cleaners dry cleaning shop clerk Lynell Murray failed to keep a date with her boyfriend, Robert Whitecotton, in Orange County. After noticing that the cleaners looked as though it had been burglarized and ransacked and that Murray's car was parked in the parking lot out back he called the police.

Murray had no idea that the previous day Marlow and Coffman saw her leaving work and that Marlow had commented that she would be "a good one to rob." The following evening at approximately 6:00 p.m., shortly before Murray was to leave work, one Lynda Schafer entered the cleaners and dropped of some clothes with Murray. Schafer would later testify that she saw Coffman "passionately embracing a man", later identified as Marlow, in an alley behind the cleaners.

At 6:30 p.m. that evening Coffman approached Linda Whitlake who was leaving her gym and asked for a ride to her motel, claiming that her car wouldn't start. After Whitlake noticed Marlow in Novis' white car with its hood up she changed her mind about giving them a ride. Coffman said that her boyfriend had decided to call the auto club instead and Whitlake left.

At 7:13 p.m. Coffman checked into room 307 of the Huntington Beach Inn under the name Lynell Murray and used Murray's credit card. At 8:19 p.m. a Bank of America branch in Corona del Mar recorded a balance inquiry into Murray's account and a subsequent withdrawal of $80 occurred, shortly followed by a $60 withdrawal, which left a balance of $4.41. Later that evening Coffman checked into the Compri Hotel in Ontario, California, with Murray's credit card. At midnight Marlow and Coffman ate dinner at the Denny's restaurant across from the hotel, which they paid for with Murray's credit card.

Murray's body would be discovered the following day at approximately 3:00 p.m. in room 307 at the Huntington Beach Inn. Her head was in the bathtub in six inches of water with it and her face bound with strips of towel. She was gagged. Her right arm was secured to her waist with a towel. Her right leg was atop the toilet and her left leg was on the floor. Her ankles looked to have been bound with duct tape as residue was evident. Her bra, nylons, and one earring were missing and she looked to have been raped and urinated on. She had also suffered pre-mortem blunt force trauma to the head, torso injuries, two black eyes, and leg bruising which were consistent with being beaten. The cause of death was determined to be ligature strangulation.

Police finally turned their attention to Marlow and Coffman after finding Novis' driver's license and checkbook in a Taco Bell takeout bag near a dumpster in Laguna Niguel along with papers with both Marlow's and Coffman's names on them. Marlow had attempted to dispose of this damning evidence but missed the dumpster. A statewide alert was issued for both Marlow and Coffman.

Arrest

On 14 November, police were dispatched to a Big Bear, California, mountain lodge after being alerted that Murray's credit card was being used to purchase clothes at a local sporting goods store. The owner of the lodge identified Marlow and Coffman as his latest guests. After finding the lodge empty, the 100-man posse discovered the suspects walking along a mountain road at approximately 3:00 p.m. They surrendered without incident, clad in clothing they had stolen from the dry cleaning shop where Murray had worked. A few hours later Coffman led police to Novis' body. One of the victim's earrings, a .22 caliber pistol and ammunition, credit card receipts with Murray's forged signature, and a Prime Cleaners paper bag with coins were found in Coffman's purse.

The Trial

Nearly three years later Marlow and Coffman would stand trial which commenced on 18 July 1989 in San Bernardino County. At several points throughout the proceedings motions for severance filed by both defendants were denied.

Among the overwhelming evidence were both defendants' fingerprints in Novis' car and that, as previously mentioned, Coffman was linked to the Fontana pawn shop where Novis' typewriter was pawned. In room 307 of the Huntington Beach Inn where Lynell Murray's body was found, a footprint on a bathmat by her body was consistent with Marlow's boots. The aforementioned Taco Bell bag with Novis' license and checkbook and documentation with Coffman's and Marlow's names was recovered. Credit card activity demonstrated where and when the defendants had used Murray's credit card. Additionally, the discarded suit jacket that Marlow had worn when they abducted Novis was found at the Bavarian Lodge and contained identification bearing Marlow's name, various single earrings presumed to be trophies from the murders, a blue ladies wallet, and the handcuffs used on Novis. Novis' vehicle was found near Santa's Village with license plates stolen from a vehicle that was at the Huntington Beach Inn and in a nearby trash can a maintenance worker found a pillowcase containing Murray's bra and laundry receipts from the cleaners where Murray had worked.

Coffman took the stand in her own behalf, painting Marlow to be an abusive man who was violent toward her and threatened both her and her son. She alleged that any violence directed toward the victims were perpetrated by Marlow. With respect to Novis, Coffman testified that on the night of Novis' death, she had dropped Novis and Marlow off at the vineyard and was told to go purchase methamphetamines. Coffman alleges that she drove a short distance, stopped and smoked a cigarette, and then returned to "the sound of digging." Marlow returned to the vehicle alone, threw some items in the back of the car, and then started to beat her for driving away.

Coffman's attorney presented numerous witnesses who corroborated Coffman's allegations of Marlow's violence including Katherine Davis, one of Marlow's ex-wives, and her mother Marlene Boggs; Coffman's former employers in Arizona; Coffman's mother Carol Maender; and clinical psychologist Craig Rath who claimed that Coffman's relationship with Marlow was "precipitated by impaired bonding in her early life", that she was not malingering, and that she did not suffer from antisocial personality disorder.

In Marlow's defense, his sister Veronica Koppers testified about the abuse and neglect the two suffered at the hands of their mother and her father Wendell Hill; about how her father shot her mother and her mother stabbed her father seven times which prompted Doris to move to California in 1963; about visiting her mother at the Sybil Brand Institute for Women and the Frontera State Prison; about how Doris introduced her daughter to drugs much like she did with Marlow and taught her how to burglarize houses; and about the myriad drinking and drug parties hosted at their house. Several witnesses at the trial testified that Doris rarely even mentioned that she had children and paid them little attention when they were together. Despite Marlow claiming responsibility for the murder in Kentucky as well as Novis' and Murray's in California he tried to shift the majority of blame onto Coffman much as she attempted to do to him.

Throughout the trial, Coffman's legal team tried to utilize the "Patty Hearst" defense that she was brainwashed, starved, and the victim of battered women's syndrome who was subjected to frequent physical, emotional, and mental abuse. Once, she claimed, Marlow beat her with a motorcycle clutch plate bruising her face and another time kicked her with his steel-toed boots. She stated that she feared for both her life and that of her then-six-year old son. Coffman's side even presented an expert on battered women's syndrome; however, the jury apparently rejected such claims.

Other testimony suggested that Coffman was the true ringleader and cold, calculated murderess, being far more intelligent than Marlow who would do anything to keep her. At one point, prosecutor Robert Gannon asked Coffman whether her relationship with Marlow was more important than the lives of Corinna Novis and Lynell Murray to which she replied, "Yes."

Sentencing

Both defendants were convicted of the kidnapping, robbery, kidnapping for robbery, residential burglary, forcible sodomy, and murder of Novis and subsequently sentenced to death on 30 August 1989. Coffman became the first women sentenced to death in California since the state reinstated capital punishment in 1977; however, California's reputation as an overly liberal state makes it unlikely that Coffman will ever be put to death.

On 8 March 1992 Marlow received a second death sentence for Murray's murder while Coffman received a life without the possibility of parole sentence added to her death sentence, the former rather moot.

On 19 August 2004 the California Supreme Court unanimously upheld both Marlow's and Coffman's death sentences.

Post-conviction

There continues to be speculation as to whether Coffman controlled or was controlled by Marlow. In fact, while on Death Row, Marlow wrote *I Wish You Were Never Born*, a novel detailing Coffman's and his murderous spree (proceeds of the sale of his book are donated to help abused children). He asserts that their story in the popular media—including an episode of *Wicked Attractions*—was sensationalized and he wanted the truth to be known.

House of Horror : The True Story of Rosemary West

75

Mary Gilmore

Unfortunately, it's not unusual in this day and time to turn on the news and hear a warning about a new serial killer roaming our streets. It's horrifying and hard to comprehend what could possibly make a person commit such heinous crimes. What is wrong with this person that drives him or her to commit such an act? The truth is that people have searched for the answers to that question for a very long time. Unfortunately, it still remains a mystery for the most part.

Rosemary West is one of those baffling cases. We will look deeper into her life and learn how her inner demons progressed to becoming one of Britain's most notorious and sadistic serial killers, taking the lives of at least 10 young women and girls.

Most of the information obtained by the authorities came from her husband and partner in crime, victims who escaped or were permitted to leave, and a great deal from her own children. Rosemary has offered very limited insight into the story, even to this day.

Remarkably, she did not act alone in committing these grisly deeds. This story is immensely complex, which I will attempt to sort out and then tie it all together with the union of Rose Letts West and Fred West in their vicious killing spree. There will be accounts of child abuse, rape, sexual deviance, torture, and murder. Rosemary West's crimes were so horrendous; it may be difficult for some of you to read.

Rosemary West's Early Life

Rosemary's mother came into her room one morning to wake her for school. Rosemary probably knew by the familiar expression on her mother's face that this would be one of those mornings that fills her life with constant dread. As she gets dressed, she begins preparing herself for what she knows is probably about to occur.

As she walks into the kitchen, breakfast is the last thing on her mind. Instead, she braces herself for the punishment she is about to receive. Don't misunderstand, Rosemary hadn't done anything wrong, but her father didn't need a reason.

His kind of punishment wasn't a time-out or a swat on the behind as most children receive. His were the kind that affect a child for a lifetime. Rose has no idea whether she is about to be beaten or if she'll endure other horrors that her father is known to inflict.

That is a likely scenario in the life of Rosemary West. Her father was a paranoid schizophrenic. The mental illness along with other problems, made life for her, her mother, and her siblings a nightmare. The abuse was bad enough, but what made it even more terrifying was not knowing from one minute to the next when or why her father's rage would erupt.

As a result of her home life, Rose made bad grades and became overweight. To make her situation worse, she was teased and bullied at school, giving her no relief from the continuous damage to her self-esteem.

There's a possibility that Rosemary's destiny was sealed much earlier in her life. It's not surprising that Rosemary's mother suffered from severe depression. The illness was so debilitating that she received electroconvulsive therapy several times while Rosemary was still in the womb, one of which occurred just before Rosemary's birth. There were some that thought this therapy was the reason for Rosemary's frequent outbursts of anger as well as her inability to do well in school.

Most of us would be unable to imagine a childhood such as the one led by Rosemary West.

Why do They Kill?

There are no exact traits of a serial killer to help us understand what drives them to kill. Some of them come from a two parent loving home while others have divorced parents. Some had abusive parents and others had loving parents.

Some think it's due to a head or brain injury sometime in their life; however, most people that have had brain injuries do not become killers. The majority of serial killers are men who act alone. Rosemary is not only a woman, she also had a partner in her life of crimes. Female killers and couples represent only a small percentage of serial killings.

The Federal Bureau of Investigation did a symposium, which was comprised of 135 experts who have dealt with serial killers in various ways to determine commonalities of serial killings. They determined that there are no definitive common traits. However, the central nervous system is constantly developing in adolescence, which determines a person's social coping system. That is, they develop the way they interact with their peers such as in negotiation and compromise. If it does not develop adequately, it can result in violent behavior.

It would be safe to say that the events of Rosemary West's childhood could be a factor in the choices she made later in life.

Rosemary's Life Before the Murders

Rosemary Letts was the fifth child born to Bill and Daisy Letts in Devon, England on the 29th of November in 1953. She normally went by the shorter version of her name, Rose. As we've seen, Rose's childhood was unlike most other children's. In pictures of Rose at a younger age she had an ever present smile on her face. You wouldn't guess that she was going through hell within the walls of her home.

The Letts family lived in Northam, a charming seaside town in Devon. Neighbors thought of Bill Letts as a nice man; however, they must have thought it strange that they rarely saw his children. When they did, the children were mainly seen walking around in their garden. One neighbor stated that they really didn't seem to be playing at all. They were just walking around and rarely seen outside the walls of the garden.

What they didn't know was that the children weren't allowed outside the walls and were afraid to play because they were forbidden to get dirty.

Although Rose's father constantly punished the children including Rose, he was not as physically abusive with Rose as with his wife and the other children. It was thought that he didn't physically abuse her as much as the others because he thought there was something not quite right about her.

Some people thought that he didn't hurt Rose as much because he was using her for his sexual pleasures instead. Others speculated that Rose learned at a very young age that she could control her father's anger by using sex.

Rose's mother Daisy, eventually left her father. She moved out of their house taking Rose and the other children with her, freeing them from the abusive environment. Remarkably, after a brief time, Rose moved back in with her father who resumed sexually abusing her.

One day, as Rose waited for a bus, she was approached by a man. Rose described him as a dirty man who had disgusting green teeth. She and the man struck up a conversation and even though his appearance was repulsive by most people's standards, Rose became attracted to him. The man's name was Fred West.

West was raising his daughter and stepdaughter at that time so Rose began babysitting the two girls. In addition, Rose and Fred also became a couple.

Fred's Early Years

Fred West, the son of Walter and Daisy West, was born in Much Marcle, England in 1941. He was the second of their six children. Growing up, he was considered to be a nice boy. They appeared to be a normal family, however, Fred's upbringing was perhaps even worse than Rosemary's. According to Fred, the motto around his house by his father was, "Do whatever you want, just don't get caught."

Fred would later reveal to police that incest was a common occurrence in his household. He said his father regularly had sex with his own daughters. Fred also claimed that his father introduced him to bestiality. In addition, it was thought that his mother Daisy took his virginity when he was 12-years-old.

Not surprising, Fred did not do well in school and dropped out at the age of 15. Two years later, he was involved in a tragic motorcycle accident. He received a broken arm and leg and a fractured skull. The head injury put him in a coma for eight days. Afterward, his family claimed that thereafter, he frequently become enraged without warning. Amazingly, two years later, he received another head injury. In this instance, he fell from a fire escape causing unconsciousness for 24 hours.

Fred's history of child abuse and head injuries would certainly coincide with the conceivable characteristics of a serial killer.

At the age of 20, he was caught and arrested for molesting a 13-year-old girl who subsequently became pregnant. He was convicted, but for unknown reasons he was not sentenced to prison. The reason is possibly because the girl's parents and Fred's parents were friends. Even with his family's propensity for deviant sexual acts, they had recently decided to try their hand at getting religion, therefore, they disowned Fred after this latest incident.

Fred had problems keeping a normal job. He landed a construction job; however, he was caught stealing. In addition, he continued to get caught molesting more young girls. It's amazing how he could still be roaming the streets even back at that point.

Shortly after, when West was around 21, he ran into a former girlfriend named Catherine Costello. She was better known as Rena, which was the name she used while prostituting and the name stuck. In addition, Rena was an accomplished thief. Nevertheless, even with her reputation, she was described by neighbors and other acquaintances as a very nice person and an exceptionally good mother.

Even though she was already pregnant with another man's child at the time, things heated up between her and Fred again and they married about two months later. The baby girl was born in February

1963 and was named Charmaine. Rena had another child by Fred a year later and named her Anna Marie. You will hear the names of these two girls in a shocking context later in the story.

Unbelievably, someone gave Fred West a job driving an ice cream van. This wouldn't seem a proper job for Fred the child molester to say the least. For Fred, it was the perfect job with young girls running after him. It was an ideal way for him to find victims.

While working at this job, a four-year-old boy ran into the street in front of his van and the child was killed. After this incident, even though the death was accidental, Fred feared people in the area would seek retribution for the boy's death. He thought it would be in his best interest to move away.

At the time, a woman named Isa McNeil was caring for the West's children. Additionally, Rena had become friends with a young woman named Anne McFall. They all moved with Fred to *The Lakeside* caravan park in Bishop's Cleeve, Gloucestershire, which is where Fred would later live with Rose.

With Fred's sadistic habits still intact, there were soon problems in this odd household. Fred insistently pushed his warped sexual necessities onto all three women. It became too much for his wife, Rena, and the children's nanny, McNeil, so the two of them moved to Scotland. On the other hand, the other woman, Ann McFall, had warmed up to Fred and stayed behind. Besides, she had already become impregnated by him.

Fearful of Fred, Rena and Isa's planned was to keep their departure secret from him and sneak away. Unfortunately, McFall told Fred, which enraged him. He allowed them to leave, but not with the two children, so the two women fled to Scotland. Rena returned frequently to visit her children.

After that, McFall began to pressure Fred to divorce Rena and marry her. Apparently, this didn't set well with Fred. When she was eight months pregnant with Fred's child, she completely vanished. She was never reported missing, but her body was later discovered in a field minus her fingers and toes, which had been removed and were missing.

Fred was left to care for his daughter and stepdaughter.

The Evil Duo Unites

Around this time is when Fred met Rose at the bus stop. It was at the time when Fred was caring for his step-daughter and biological daughter, so Fred already had at least the one murder of Anne McFall under his belt when he met Rose. Rose then began taking care of the two children.

When they first got together Rose was only 16-years-old and Fred was 12 years older at 28. Her father absolutely disapproved of the relationship. He threatened West that if he didn't leave Rose alone he would call Social Services due to Rose's young age. That was ironic since her father had been having sex with her himself for a long time. Of course, that was most likely the reason he didn't want her to go.

Nevertheless, Rose moved in with Fred and they lived together as a family with Fred's two daughters. After only about two months, they married she moved in with him at *The Lakeside Caravan Park* in Bishop's Cleeve, Gloucestershire, where Fred had lived with Rena and Anne.

Of course Fred, a man of few scruples, soon introduced his young and damaged wife to a sadistic world of pornography and urged her into prostitution. Due to Rose's demoralizing childhood, it didn't take a lot of urging for her to become caught up in his world.

Not one to hold down a regular job, Fred's contribution to the income was mainly by thievery. He wasn't very accomplished at that either and was frequently caught and arrested. It wasn't long before he was sent to prison for 10 months, leaving young Rose in charge of his two daughters.

To make matters worse, she had become pregnant and gave birth to her daughter, Heather, in 1970 while Fred was still in jail. Being young in addition to having mental problems, caring for three children was a tall order for Rose and she didn't handle the situation well, to say the least.

To add to the pressure, seven-year-old Charmaine, began to be unruly and Rose was unable to cope with it. Years later, according to the other child, Anna Marie, it was not unusual for both girls to receive severe beatings; however, no matter how bad the beating, Charmaine refused to cry. This infuriated Rose so it's no surprise that Charmaine didn't seem to be around any longer after that.

This is thought to be when Rose committed her first murder. Rose's tendency to lose her temper most likely caused her to loss control and kill Charmaine. Apparently, Rose hid the girl's body, because it's known that Fred disposed of the body after he returned from prison.

Fred would hold this over Rose in the future. On one of the occasions when Rose's father tried to convince her to leave Fred and come home, Fred made a remark that was something like, "Come on now Rose, you know what we have between us." For someone that didn't know Fred, it would sound like an expression of love. More than likely with Fred, it was his not so subtle way of saying, "You can't leave. I have too much on you." She later told her parents that Fred would do anything, including murder.

Fred's first undertaking after returning from jail was to dismembered and dispose of Charmaine's body. For whatever sick reason, as with Anne McFall, he removed her fingers and toes and then buried her. This became the normal process in Fred's body disposal. It was later speculated that Fred and Rose were possibly involved in Satan worship. It is thought by some that removing the fingers and toes of their sacrifices was typical for Satan worshipers.

The next time Rena Costello came to visit her daughter it naturally created a problem when she discovered her daughter's absence, thanks to Rose. As you can imagine, Rena was not happy about her missing daughter and demanded some answers. Therefore, Rose and Fred must have decided that Rena would have to go as well. So this visit to see her little girl resulted in Rena's demise as well. Minus her fingers and toes, she was buried in a field close to the Caravan Hotel where Rose and Fred still lived.

That meant a total of at least three people had already lost their lives courtesy of Fred and Rose West. One each for Rose and Fred and now Rena by both of them.

A brief time later, Rose gave birth to their second child, Mae. They bought a large two-story house in Gloucester; however, there was not much money coming in. Fred started putting up panels in the rooms to create multiple bedrooms called bedsits. They were tiny rooms, which didn't fit much more than a bed. They began renting out these rooms for extra income; however, the rooms served another purpose as well.

By this time, Rose's fulltime career had become *prostitute*. They also began working other women out of the house. One of the rooms labeled "Rose's Room" was dedicated to Rose for turning tricks. Outside the door was a red light, which was lit when the room was in business. The children knew they were not to disturb when the red light was on. The room also came complete with a peephole, which was Fred's method for watching his wife in action and for making videos.

Both Rose and Fred had come from a family where incest was normal. It was not unnatural to them when Rose's own father occasionally came to their house to have sex with her.

In around October of 1972, Rose and Fred hired Carol Owens as a new nanny for their children. She told her story years later stating that Fred and Rose attempted to bring her into their twisted lifestyle. Not wanting any part of it, she soon left their house.

A few weeks later, as she was walking home, Fred pulled up beside her and offered a ride. The next thing she knew he hit her on the head. When she awoke, her hands were tied and Fred was in the process of taping her mouth.

She was told that if she tried to resist, Fred would call in his friends and let them have their way with her and she would then be killed.

They said they would bury her under the paving stones outside their home along with hundreds of other girls. Terrified, she didn't attempt to resist.

Unbelievably, they allowed her to leave the next day and she proceeded to file charges on them. Fred somehow managed to convince the court that the sex was consensual. In addition, Owens decided that testifying against these two could be an unhealthy choice.

The couple was given a meager fine on a charge of indecent assault and then released. She would be the last victim that the Wests' would allow to leave alive.

Years later, she regretted not testifying. She felt that if she had, it could have saved the lives of numerous women and girls and she was most likely correct.

One day, Fred and Rose arrived home and their neighbor, Elizabeth Agius, was outside. She had become friendly with the couple, so Fred stopped for a chat. Just in conversation, she asked what they had been doing, so Fred proceeded to tell her exactly what they had been up to.

He said they were cruising around looking for young girls. He must have felt he needed to explain why his wife would go along with him on such an outing. He said they figured the girls would see Rose and wouldn't be scared to get in the car. She would later say that she thought he must be joking...he wasn't.

Meanwhile, Fred was busy redecorating the cellar. One of the prostitutes that worked in the house later told authorities that she saw black suits, masks, chains, and whips down there. Fred had created his own torture chamber.

Anna Marie, Fred's remaining child with Rena Costello, was the first to be brutalized in Fred's torture chamber. She was bound, gagged, and violently raped as Rose watched. She was only eight-years-old at the time and this treatment would continue for years.

Eventually, Anna Marie moved out of the house to live with her boyfriend, which quite possibly saved her life. Again, letting her go would prove to be a bad move for the Wests later in court. As one of the survivors, a considerable amount of the horror stories came from her.

After Anna Marie's departure, Fred's attentions naturally turned to his daughters Heather and Mae; however, Heather wanted no part of it and resisted. Understandably, she was unable to keep it to herself and told a friend about the horrors happening at home. This would seal her fate, but Fred later claimed to police that her death was accidental.

The life of Rose and Fred West continued filled with the unimaginable. They would go on to have a total of seven children who were born in a short time span. It is believed that three are by Fred, one is by her own father, and the remaining three are from her clients. It almost seemed that their reason for having children was so Fred and Rose would have someone to torture at the times when no one else was tied up in the cellar. You can certainly say with certainty that Fred and Rose West were definitely not loving parents.

The One's That Didn't Survive the Terror

Over the next few years, the abuse of the West's children continued as did the murders of others. At some point, Fred went to work at a slaughter house. It was thought that this is when his already violent habits became even more gruesome. It could have been a factor in his fascination for dismembering his victims.

It is believed the next victim was Lynda Gough who was a personal acquaintance of the West's. She enjoyed participating in some of their sexual activities by sharing sex partners with Rose. However, for unknown reasons she later vanished. Gough's mother came to the West's house looking her daughter and was told that she moved in order to pursue a job. While she was speaking to the woman, Rose was wearing some of Linda Gough's clothing.

Carol Ann Cooper, only 15-years-old, is thought to be the next victim. She disappeared while walking home from the movies.

Evidence showed she died by strangulation, was dismembered, and buried in the garden.

Lucy Partington was in town visiting her family and a friend over the Christmas holidays. She went to the bus station to take a bus back home and most likely Fred, being one to hang out at bus stations asked her if she wanted a ride. As Fred and Rose planned, it is thought that the only reason she let them even approached her was due to the presence of Rose.

It is thought that they kept Partington in captivity for about a week after she vanished because poor Fred showed up at the hospital about a week later with a large laceration needing stitches. Authorities think he received the cut while cutting up Partington.

Shirley Hubbard went missing when she was returning home from Droitwich. There was definitive evidence of her torture. Her head was completely wrapped with tape with only a short rubber tube in her mouth to breath.

Juanita Marian Mott was a former tenant of the Wests'. Her torture was obvious. She was gagged with a binding made of socks, tights, and a bra, which were all stuffed inside each other. She was also tied up with clothes line rope looped around her thighs, arms, wrists, and ankles. This was done with the rope going back and forth around her horizontally and vertically until she was completely immobilized. She also had a rope with a noose, which most likely suspended her from the rafters in the cellar.

Shirley Anne Robinson was one of the prostitutes that worked out of their house who had sexual relations with both Fred and Rose. She became pregnant by Fred, at the same time Rose was pregnant by one of her clients.

Shirley began to get the idea she would like to replace Rose, which is not advisable in this family. Rose demanded that she had to go. She and her unborn child were dismembered and buried in the back garden. The cellar was full of bodies by this time and the back garden became the new burial grounds.

Therese Siegenthaler was a hitchhiker in route from London to Ireland. Some of the evidence showed that like Partington, she was kept alive for close to a week during which time she was likely tortured and raped.

Allison Chambers was the last known non-related victim. She was killed in 1979.

Their oldest daughter, Heather Ann West, was the last known victim. Fred claims he killed her by accident. His story of the "accident" went something like this. He told police that Heather was being extremely insolent so he had to slap her. She then started laughing at him so he was forced to grab her by the throat to stop her from laughing. He said that unfortunately, he must have grabbed her too tightly because she began to turn blue and stopped breathing. He tried to revive her by putting her in the tub and running cold water on her, but it didn't work.

He then removed her clothes and attempted to put her in a garbage bin, but she didn't fit. Back into the tub she went so he could make her smaller, but he first strangled her with a cord to make sure she was dead. He told police he didn't want to start cutting her up and then have her come alive on him.

He also closed her eyes before he started cutting. He said he couldn't dismember her while she was looking at him. He must have been hearing a strange sound because he told police he found the source of a noise when he cut off her head. He said it was a horrible and unpleasant sound like scrunching. He also said that after cutting her up, she fit quite nicely into the garbage bin.

She was later put in a hole that the West's son, Stephen, had dug with the intention of it becoming a fishpond. Fred put Heather in the hole and built a patio over it. Stephen had unknowingly dug the grave for his own sister's burial.

Police also believed that they killed 15-year-old Mary Bastholm in 1968, though they never found her body. The Wests' son Stephen, later told authorities that he believes Bastholm was one of his father's earlier murders because his father boasted about it.

The Evidence Begins to Surface

Oddly, they violently murdered many of their victims, but then set others free after they had finished using and abusing them. Naturally, some of them went to the police.

The released victims were some extremely lucky women to say the least. Their reports finally got the attention of a Detective Constable named Hazel Savage. Savage was also familiar with Fred West and his arrests for thievery and child molestation through the years since the time he was married to Rena Costello.

Fred videoed an incident in which he raped Anna Marie while Rose held her arms. Anna Marie told friends about her home life who in turn told their parents. This and other information got back to Savage.

This enabled the Detective to obtain a warrant to search the West's property. It was the beginning of the needed evidence to finally remove these damaged and dangerous monsters from the unsuspecting public.

Fred was arrested and charged with rape and sodomy of a minor and Rose for assisting in the rape of a minor. Amazingly, Fred and Rose West were still not suspected of murder. At this time, the younger children were removed from the home.

Due to the evidence found in the home, Detective Savage had the suspicion that there was more going on here and she began digging deeper into this strange family. She had a feeling that there was something suspicious concerning the whereabouts of their daughter Heather and she was determined to find out.

For instance, it was noticed in the videos of the West's and their children that was seized from their home that Heather was never present. Also, in interviews with some of the children, they said something that should not come from the mouths of children.

Apparently, there was a common joke around the West house. Fred told the children that he would buried them under the patio with their sister Heather if they didn't behave.

Unbelievably, the case fell apart when two of the main witnesses decided not to testify. Detective Savage continued questioning the children repeatedly to no avail. Fred and Rose had programmed them and put enough fear in them by then that they would no longer say anything to help the case.

However, the evidence together with case workers reporting the family joke about their sister Heather kept Detective Savage searching. It also appeared that another child, Charmaine, was missing as well. Eventually, Savage put together enough evidence to obtain a warrant to dig on the Wests' property.

Soon after that, Rose answered the door to find the police with warrant in hand. She quickly called Fred to tell him the police were about to dig on their property and they're looking for Heather. It turned out that Fred would be of little help because it took him four hours to get home. He came up with some excuse about passing out due to inhaling paint fumes at work.

Could it have been that Fred was busy disposing of evidence such as fingers and toes or perhaps he had a burial he had not gotten around to completing. That will never be determined.

They began searching the house in addition to excavating the garden in February 24, 1994. The dig was originally intended to search for the body of the daughter Heather, which they soon found. Fred was brought in by the police for questioning the next day. He surprised the police by confessing to the murder of his daughter Heather and he repeatedly told police that Rose knew nothing about it.

Fred and Rose must have been up all that night getting their stories straight. It is thought that Fred assured Rose he would take all the blame and she shouldn't worry. Fred was good to his word, at least in the beginning.

Meanwhile, after the attending pathologist began inspecting the bones of Heather, he brought it to the attention of the police that there was an extra leg bone indicating the presence of at least one other body.

After that discovery, Fred decided he should do some damage control by telling police the location of Alison Chambers and Shirley Robinson's bodies. He hoped this would prevent them from doing any more digging.

It was first thought that Fred did this to avoid being categorized a serial killer, which is someone that kills more than three people. Unbelievably, as it turned out, Fred wanted the police to stop digging because he didn't want his cherished home to be torn apart any further.

Nevertheless, they continued and began to find more human bones. Rose was not arrested until around March 4, 1994. Even then, it was only for sex offenses. Fred had trouble deciding for sure if he wanted to protect Rose after all. He would go on the recant his confession that he killed Heather and then later changed his mind again saying Rose was innocent.

In Britain, prisoners are sometimes assigned an "appropriate adult", which is someone that assists and basically befriends the prisoner. This was normally done for juveniles; however, Janet Leach was assigned to Fred. Leach didn't know she was about to become the confidant of a serial killer.

It turned out that Fred became comfortable enough with Leach that he soon told her the whole gory story. She pointblank asked him if there were more victims. Fred responded that there were six more and went on to draw a sketch of his house and garden complete with the locations of the graves.

Fred knew exactly where they were located; however, he had some trouble remembering all their names. He recalled one that had a scar on her hand; therefore, Scar Hand became her name. Another he called Tulip because he thought she was Dutch, although she was actually Swiss.

Fred was now on a roll and confessed to the murders of his ex-wife Rena Costello and ex-lover, Anne McFall. He told leach that he dumped them nearby his childhood home. He then confessed that he buried his step-daughter Charmaine, Fred's child that Rose killed, close to the hotel where they lived in Gloucester. Strangely, Fred would admit to the murders, but he would not admit to the rapes.

Meanwhile, Rose continued to play the role of an innocent woman, denying any involvement in the murders. She went so far as to act horrified at the actions of her perverted husband. When Fred attempted to contact her, she snubbed him not wanting to have anything to do with such a despicable person.

After making bail, Rose moved into a halfway house with her son Stephen and her daughter Mae. The police were not convinced of her innocence and bugged the house. Nevertheless, Rose stuck to it and never spoke of anything that would involve her in murder. Only charges of sexual offense remained against her.

As can be imagined, the town of Gloucester was flooded with the media. The attention had a tremendous impact on the small town. The West's house became known by the appropriate name "The House of Horrors". The residents were in disbelief that this unimaginable crime spree had gone on in their town for 20 years.

The Trial

As it turned out, Fred took the easy way out. He hanged himself in his jail cell by tying together bed sheets leaving Rose to deal with the whole state of affairs.

She was finally charged with 10 of the murders since Rena Costello and Anne McFall were before she was on the scene. She went to trial in October of 1995.

One after another, witnesses took the stand and told their shocking stories. One of the highest drama moments of the trial came with the testimony of Fred's oldest daughter, Anna Marie. She was on the stand for two days. At one point she looked her stepmother straight in the eye as she told a story of sexual abuse and torture that began when she was a little girl of only eight-years-old.

She recalled the incident when she was so savagely raped by her father while Rose held her arms. During the incident, Rose was telling her how lucky she was to have parents to show her how to please her husband when she gets married. She said she was hurt so badly that she couldn't attend school for several days. She also recalled a day that her father strapped her down and raped her while he was home for a quick lunch break. These were only two of the many horror stories she lived.

The second day of her testimony was delayed for several hours because she took an overdose of pills the previous evening.

Another person that offered a wealth of damaging testimony was Fred's *Appropriate Adult* and confidant, Janet Leach. However, she became so stressed that she suffered a stroke during the trial causing another delay. It wasn't until later after the trial's end that Leach could tell police the entire story that Fred confided in her.

One of the key witnesses was Carol Owens who was one of the girls they brought home under the pretense of being a nanny. She was allowed to leave, but only after she endured their sadistic sexual torture. Needless to say, she had tales to tell.

Another witness who is still referred to as Miss A was lured to the West house and saw two naked girls who were being held prisoner. She watched as they were tortured and raped. She was then raped by Fred and sexually assaulted by Rose. She was one of the lucky ones that left that cellar with her life.

It wasn't hard for the jury to come back with a unanimous verdict of guilty on 10 counts of murder. Rose received life in prison.

The Aftermath

The "House of Horrors" at 25 Cromwell Street in Gloucester where nine bodies were found was demolished in October of 1996; however, there seemed to be a curse that affected many of the people associated with Rose and Fred West.

John West, Fred's brother, hanged himself while awaiting his trial for the rape of his own niece Anna Marie.

Anna Marie continued to suffer from the memories of her distorted childhood. In 1999, she attempted suicide by jumping from a bridge. She was rescued, leaving her to live another day with the memory of the horrors from her past.

Stephen West, the son of Rose and Fred, attempted to commit suicide in 2002 in the same manner as his father and uncle by hanging himself. However, it wasn't meant to be because the rope broke.

The actual number of murders will remain a mystery. During his interrogation by the police, Fred stated that there were two more bodies buried in shallow graves that they would never find.

He also told them there were 20 other bodies spread around in various places. He claimed he would show the police the location of one body each year. One wonders if he knew at that time that he would later take his own life and wouldn't be following through with that promise.

Fred took any other secrets he had in his evil little mind with him to his grave. After that, Rose wasn't interested in discussing the matter any further.

According to an article in DailyMail.com[1] dated February 2014, even though Rose West filed for a couple of appeals after she went to prison, she has now decided she never wants to leave her top security jail cell at Low Newton jail in Durham and why would she, her cell is equipped with TV, radio, CD player, and private bathroom. She has never confessed to committing any murders.

Authorities know the women and girls were tortured, raped, killed, dismembered, and buried; however, they don't know the details of many of those crimes. Rose has been asked by numerous people to give those details, but she refuses.

---

1.   http://www.dailymail.co.uk/news/article-2565316/Avon-Monopoly-The-Archers-Why-Rose-West-loves-life-jail.html

Conclusion

This is an account of actual facts; however, it hard to believe that it's anything other than a fictional horror story.

Even after hearing about the disturbing childhoods of both Rose and Fred West, it's difficult to understand the extent of their warped minds. Even more disturbing is the fact that two people that are this broken can find one another and carry out their evil deeds together.

This story brings us no closer to the answer of what drives serial killers. Both Rose and Fred were abused as children mainly by their fathers; however, it was young women and girls that were the focus of their punishment.

There have been books and a movie made about them to show us how this horrific story unfolds. However, only in our minds can we come close to conjuring up the evil that occurred within the walls of 25 Cromwell Street. We may never know the full extent of the terrors that transpired.

The fact that Fred West is gone and Rose West will never see the light of day should make us all sleep a little more soundly.

THE COLD CASE OF LEAH ROBERTS

96

CHELSEA CROSS

When a loved one goes missing, the people closest to them who find themselves left behind often become consumed with the task of finding them. It is a relief to discover them, alive or dead, because then the mystery is solved, at least in part. However, when a person disappears and has yet to be found, what remains in place of them are the unanswered questions, worries, and strong emotions such as rage, guilt, sorrow, or unfathomable loneliness. The case of Leah Robert's is but one example of a missing person's case turned cold, with no new leads despite national attention and multiple re-dramatizations on shows like Unsolved Mysteries and Investigation Discovery. Her older sister and brother, Kara and Heath Roberts, are still searching for her although nearly seventeen years have gone by since her disappearance. Hopefully, someday soon, they will find answers.

Leah's white 1993 Jeep Cherokee had been found on March 18th, 2000. Some sources state that the vehicle was an SUV, which is a common contradiction in this case. Depending on which source you read can even affect how you feel about Leah as a person. With many unanswered questions, people have a natural tendency to fill in the blanks themselves. There were many clues in and around the Leah's vehicle, where her personal affects had been scattered about and left behind, but there was no sign of Leah. There are just as many unknowns as there are hints about what happened to her and where she could be. Among all the other mysterious circumstances surrounding her disappearance, there are hints of Jack Kerouac's influence. Kerouac, who was a Beat Generation novelist, is best known for *On the Road*, although Leah was also a big fan of another work of his known as *The Dharma Bums*. The latter novel depicts scenes of the area where her jeep was found and the former novel described a life of freedom from constraints, which begs the question: how closely might Leah have been trying to follow Kerouac's lead? Or was her presence in the area the product of something more sinister?

Her brother and sister might spend the rest of their lives looking for closure in their sister's disappearance. There is still a reward of $10,000 being offered for further information. Her siblings and the organization they have partnered with, Community United Effort, believe that even the coldest cases can be solved. It is important to remember that the answers might be difficult to hear: was Leah Roberts a victim of a kidnapping or murder? Was she mentally ill and simply lost herself in the expanses of a Washington forest or had she intentionally committed suicide? The evidence in her jeep, at least, tells us that she was not killed in the wreckage of her car, and so perhaps she managed to escaped a total of two car crashes during her life. However, by the time that her jeep had rolled several times over down a steep hill and into the forest, Leah Roberts may have already been dead. It is impossible to know for sure without someone coming forward with more details.

Early Life

Leah Toby Roberts had blue eyes and sandy blonde hair. She did not have an easy life. Although her childhood seemed normal for that part of Durham, North Carolina: a loving family with two siblings, Heath and Kara, for her to squabble and play together. Her grade school life also seemed average, and she obtained good enough grades to get accepted into North Carolina State University, which is when the first of the many tragedies in their lives struck: her family learned that her father had a serious, chronic lung illness. She was seventeen at the time, and despite the dark news, she was able to maintain her grades and stay in school that year. When she was twenty and working at completing her sophomore year at university, the second family tragedy struck: heart disease claimed her mother's life unexpectedly. In order to grieve and adjust to life after her mother, Leah took some time off of school. Shortly after returning to school in 1998, Leah was in a horrific car accident, in which her lung was punctured and her femur was shattered. She had an identifying surgical scar on her hip where a metal rod had been inserted in order to help the bone growth of her femur. When she awoke in the hospital, she claimed that she had gained a new lease on life. In order to recover, she again left school for a short time.

After these three bleak events shook up her life, Leah managed to press on with a new verve. She continued her education in Spanish and Anthropology, and was set to go to Costa Rica for a field program in order to obtain higher fluency in Spanish. It was at that time that the final tragedy in her early twenties occurred. Her father died mere weeks before she was set to leave the country. However, she doggedly continued to prepare and leave for her trip, while leaving her mourning siblings behind to care for the estate. After the field program concluded, Leah spent a little longer in school before deciding that she would discontinue her program just before beginning her final semester. Both of her siblings urged her to stay in school for the final six months, but she could not be persuaded. Heath told reporters that he thought "that all of those things together had the cumulative effect of making Leah even more introspective and probably more aware that, although she didn't know what she wanted to do, I think she was unhappy that she wasn't achieving it." Her sister Kara, on the *Larry King Live* show, said to the audience and viewers that by "the time Leah was 22 she had lost both of her parents and here she is on the verge of graduating from college and I think she just felt lost and didn't have a lot of direction, and I feel like this took this trip as a soul-searching trip." A friend of hers named Susie Smith reported that "Leah is just a very awesome person. Everybody that meets her likes her. Very personable, great smile. But, you know, she was kind of private also. Definitely." These three comments paint a picture of an intelligent, insightful, and kindhearted young woman who was experiencing deep agony. Instead of staying in school, Leah seemed to completely turn her life direction around. She decided to pick up photography and guitar, adopting a kitten, and writing poetry in local coffeehouses. Somewhere in this time,

Leah began to discuss her fondness for the novelist Jack Kerouac.

Road Trip and Disappearance

Shortly after she began to frequent the local coffee shop with her poetry, she made new friends such as Jeannine Quiller and her roommate, Nicole Bennett. Leah often discussed taking a trip like the ones detailed in Kerouac's novels with the other young women. Jeannine has said that "from the last conversation that we had, we were talking about *Dharma Bums* and about how Kerouac was up on Desolation Peak, just taking in all the beauty around him." This was the dream trip that her sister Kara now suspects was Leah's attempt to soul-search as she tried to recover from the five year span of shocking events and sudden losses. During her stints at the coffee shop, she wrote a lot of poetry, and she spent much of her time there reflecting on the meaning of life. Finally, in March, Leah and Kara had spoken to each other on the phone about what they were hopeful about in the coming year. Throughout this conversation, Kara felt that things looked like they were coming around for Leah. Kara recollects that the two sisters had committed to seeing each other in the coming week when the phone call ended.

Around the same time as that phone call, on March 9th, Leah and Nicole applied for a babysitting gig they would need to be at the following day. After that, Nicole left for work, and by the time she returned home, Leah's jeep was gone. Without school or a job, Leah's schedule had been sporadic, so Nicole did not become suspicious until Leah missed the babysitting shift the next day. Leah went unheard from on March 11th, again on March 12th, until finally, she was reported missing to the Durham police on March 13th by Kara.

Kara and Nicole went through Leah's belongings on March 14th in order to find some hints about where she might be. They found a note left by Leah that said: "I'm not suicidal. I'm the opposite. Remember Jack Kerouac." To end the note, Leah had drawn a Cheshire Cat's grin, which hadn't garnered any sort of significance in the press, even now. The other unusual part of the note is that Leah had left it in her room in plain sight, but not on the kitchen counter or on the fridge. For some reason, Leah had assumed that someone would be going into her room or through her possessions. This is also where she left her portion of the rent for the upcoming month. Among the missing was Leah's kitten, although no one knew for sure whether or not Leah had taken her along until later. During her trip to Costa Rica, Leah had given Kara the power of attorney over her bank accounts, which Kara also used to try and determine what was going on with her sister. There were gas station entries as well as motel rooms and other small purchases and larger cash withdrawals, which traced a trail to the northwest. However, after the card was used to buy gas on the 13th, the usage of the card stopped. Despite no new purchases, at that time no one had any reason to suspect that Leah had met with foul play. Once Kara came into contact with Leah's friend Jeannine and spoken to her about their mutual love for Kerouac, Kara felt reassured that she knew Leah's plan and went back to her own day to day life. However, on March 18th, Kara expected a Happy Birthday phone call from Leah, but never received it. Instead, on that day, she received a letter from the Durham County sheriff's office in her door's mailbox with instructions to call the Whatcom County Sheriff's office in Bellingham, Washington. Upon making that call, Kara was suddenly faced with the fifth tragedy in her young life. After her father's diagnosis, her mother's death, Leah's car accident, her father's death, Kara now had to deal with Leah's disappearance and potential death or suicide.

The car was discovered by two joggers who came upon several articles of clothing tied in trees, although some sources allege that the clothing was merely hanging off of the tree branches. They then followed the scattered clothing along a trail down a treacherous embankment to a white jeep, which was in poor condition. It was off the side of a small road named Canyon Creek Road, which connected to the Mount Baker Highway, which leads to some residences and logging camps at the base and throughout the Mount Baker-Snoqualmie National Forest, which is located a small ways south of the US-Canadian border. Leah was not there when the jeep was discovered, the jogging couple had not seen any signs of her in the area besides the strangely placed articles of clothing. Kara and Heath flew out to meet investigators in Bellingham in order to aid with the search and further investigation.

The Investigation

The jeep had been traveling approximately 40 miles an hour when it left Canyon Creek Road and crashed into the forest. Investigators were able to determine the speed of the vehicle by examining the damage done to it and the nearby vegetation. The insides of the jeep had clothing and pillows set up and placed about as if the vehicle had been used as some sort of shelter, however, the other contents were thrown around and jumbled up, which are traits of a multiple rollover event. Kevin McFadden of the Whatcom County Sheriff's Office said that the driver should have been injured: "With the speed that the vehicle was traveling and the amount of damage to the vehicle, you would anticipate some type of injury to the person inside. At least some type of evidence to indicate contact damage, that the person had been inside the vehicle ... we brought in dogs, we brought in search and rescue, and did a complete grid search up and down the road. But they weren't able to find any indication that anybody had left that vehicle." For some reason, someone had placed the pillows and clothing to form a shelter, but did not pickup the scattered belongings of Leah, some of which included quite a bit of cash ($2,500) and jewelery. Her guitar and cds were also untouched. A small cat carrier and some food were also on the sign, which indicated that Leah had brought her kitten with her. Like Leah, Bea the kitten has never been found. An important clue was found in her belongings as well, which helped investigators understand when she arrived in the area, and that was an innocuous ticket stub for the movie American Beauty on March 13th, which aired at the Bellis Fair shopping mall. That meant that Leah had purchased gas in Oregon and then spent a few hours in the town after the 5-6 hour drive. Besides the fact that her belongings were spread-out everywhere around the crash site, there were none of the signs of the blunt force trauma that normally come standard in a multiple rollover style car crash such as fractured glass or blood, however. Since then, there has been evidence found of the starter being tampered with, which lends itself to the suggestion that the vehicle was empty when the accident occurred.

After Kara and Heath arrived, they began to ask questions in the neighboring town of Bellingham and passed out papers with Leah's picture and information on them. They spoke to businesses where Leah might have gone, although the amount of cash found in her jeans pointed to her buying very little in the town. They headed to the only sit-down restaurant that the Bellis Fair Mall offered, because Kara had an instinct that Leah may have eaten there before or after seeing the movie. The restaurant management led the officers to two men, one of whom claimed that Leah had left the establishment with a man named Barry and created a sketching of him for the police. None of the other patrons or the other man could verify whether or not Leah had actually left with someone, but police did note that on the security footage obtained from that gas station in Oregon, Leah kept searching the parking lot as if someone had been waiting for her. Unfortunately, the gas station had not had security cameras monitoring their parking lot, although officers do believe that there was no one else in the car with her.

One of the biggest indicators to police that Leah had met with foul play was the engagement ring that they had found under the car mat in her car. The ring belonged to Leah's mother, and she never went without it, as it served a constant reminder of her mother. Her roommate Nicole Bennett also knows about the ring: "As long as I've known Leah, she has worn her mother's engagement ring. It was her most prized possession. And when we discovered that the ring had been found in the car, it was definitely, for me, a bad sign." Those close to Leah have gone on record as saying that she wouldn't have taken it off unless she felt she had to, or if she was completely unaware. Some have suggested that Leah may have been in a fugue state, which is officially known as Dissociative fugue and is classed as a DSM-5 Dissociative Disorder. Normally fugue shapes are temporary and last from a few hours to to days, but there are rare instances in which they can last for months. These fugue states are often accompanied with sudden travel and establishing a new identity. There is a lot of parallel between the DSM-5 definition and Leah's case, with a few small differences including the fact that Leah had planned the trip somewhat substantially. Although in Oregon she was considered to be in good shape, a man had called in a panicked sighting of Leah in Everett, Washington, which is likely when she was last seen.

What We Know Now

Since the day of the accident, the widespread area where Leah disappeared has been subject to repeat searches by cadaver dogs and metal detectors, looking for the metal rod that Leah had had put in when her femur had shattered. The *Unsolved Mystery* show aired a segment on her disappearance back in 2001, when its segment still played on Lifetime. None of the tips that came as a result of the broadcast led the investigators to anything worthwhile. Kara teamed up with Monica Caison, who is an expert in solving cold cases by drawing consistent media and national attention to them. On a now annual basis, Kara and Caison organize a caravan through Caison's organization, Community United Effort, which travels the route Leah had likely taken during her fateful trip. They both went onto the Larry King Live, and Kara told the viewers: "I don't really know how I would have made it through the past five years without [Caison] ... We're just trying to, you know, keep Leah's face out there as much as possible."

Near the time of the Investigation Discovery airing of Leah's case in 2011, two investigators had been handed the care of Leah's vehicle, which Kara had asked the police station to protect. They found new evidence that had been ignored in the original investigation. There was a male's DNA on Leah's clothing, and they were the investigators who noticed that the starter relay in the jeep had been altered. The alteration made it clear that Leah did not have to be in the car, nor no one had to be, in order for the vehicle to continue acceleration until its demise. The investigators noted that the man who had originally told investigator about the mysterious third man, named "Barry", had been a mechanic and ex-military. They began to suspect him, and they made actions to get his DNA and fingerprints examined, but he had moved to Canada in the years since the initial investigation, which made the process more difficult. By the time the *Disappearance* episode on Investigation Discovery had aired, the fingerprints had come back negative and the DNA had yet to be processed. He has allegedly commented on online forums protesting his innocence.

Kerouac's Influence on Modern Youth

Jack Kerouac's writing and lifestyle have had an obvious influence on Leah and her missing persons case. He is known as an author of the Beat Generation, and he is likely the most famous. Although his writings were largely anti-capitalistic, very quickly his novels became very popular, and the bohemian lifestyle depicted within morphed into a Hollywood-style spectacle. Years later, however, these ideas of Kerouac returned to the youth they were originally meant for, and inspired Leah to take her road trip. Even during the height of Kerouac's popularity, his ideals were heavily criticized and served as scapegoats for many of the political problems of the age. It seemed as though the thoughts expressed within *On the Road* were offending everyone who wasn't a beatnik. That said, he influenced Bob Dylan's political flare as well as newer writers and philosophers like Sven Birkerts and Thomas Pynchon. Students all over the country were reading him in the 60s and 70s, despite *On the Road* not being added to the curriculum until much later. The novel addresses the dissatisfaction with mainstream culture that some factions of America possess, and has remained as part of the cultural background ever since. Multiple editions have been published since the original, each honoring some facet of the novel—the original manuscript, for example, or a marked anniversary.

Into the 21st century, the book remains a heavy influence of counter-cultures such as hipster, dust punk, and the bohemian lifestyle, which brings us back to Leah Roberts. On the Road, among Kerouac's other works, remains a steadfast influence on the youth of today who are unable to cope with the pressures of modern American society. Although Leah was seemingly a part of the mainstream that counter-cultures reject, the sudden loss and traumas that she had experienced in such a short time span might have parallels with the pressure to achieve. Leah was maintaining her grades throughout adverse circumstances, and there is no way of telling how much pressure she was applying to herself, but the sudden decision to drop out of university so close to it being finished acknowledges that she was under considerable stress. The freedom from stressors that life on the road offered must have been very tempting for her.

Conclusion

Mysteries and missing persons' cases are equal parts thrilling and chilling because they could happen to anyone. In 2012 alone there was upwards of 700,000 missing persons cases in the United States and at any one time there are approximately 90,000 persons missing on average. Of those 90,000, two thirds are adults, and there is a relatively even gender split. About half are white, which includes Hispanic ancestry. Unlike Leah Roberts' case, however, most missing persons in the United States are found. Although the first day or two are the most integral, and it may be that Leah's case had been reported too late. It is actually rare for someone to disappear without a trace, which makes Leah's case all the more unusual and frightening. Perhaps if she had kept a more regular schedule, her friends and family may have been more concerned about her road trip. Her face remains a national news icon, and her sister and brother are still actively searching for her, even if her file has gone cold. It is hard to answer why she hasn't been found yet, and there are still too many unsolved riddles regarding her disappearance.

Leah had many reasons to be depressed or mentally ill, but so did her sister and brother. It is likely that she did not commit suicide, but the possibility is still there. Why did she suddenly drop out of university? Up until then, she seemed to be a highly motivated individual, despite having to miss a few semesters of school due to personal tragedies. The investigators have gone on record saying that "you can't rule out foul play when you don't see somebody for over a year, but there's no evidence to indicate that that has happened. We did process the vehicle for your typical evidence, hairs and fibers and blood, but there was nothing to indicate that happened." Could Leah have been kidnapped or murdered a long ways away from her vehicle and the crash site? Many online commenters suggest that perhaps Leah made herself a new person and has kept out of the national spotlight, despite how difficult that would be in the modern age and considering that her attempt to disappear would have been most likely caused by a fugue state. Some have suggested that Leah wanted to live as free as Kerouac did within his novels, although her sister Kara doubts that theory: "I can understand Leah's needing to get away and find some peace within herself, but considering the loss that our family's experienced, it's difficult for me to think that she would leave us open for another loss like this." Likely, Leah wanted a Kerouac-inspired vacation from her society and instead she met with yet another horrible tragedy.

SPREE KILLER: THE TRUE STORY OF AMY BISHOP

112

ANNA MASON

Amy Bishop Biography

When you think about school shootings, the first thing that will come to mind is troubled students going on a killing spree and murdering their peers without any good reason. Even though similar crimes happened numerous times in the past, the thorough coverage of Columbine turned school shootings into worldwide news. The experts started to recognize it as a real problem because the frequency increased after 1999 even though the security at schools and universities improved greatly. But what happens when a renowned professor snaps, pulls out their gun, and start killing their colleagues?

This is exactly what happened in University of Alabama in Huntsville back in February of 2010. Amy Bishop, a biology professor who seemed perfectly fine on the outside decided to attack the faculty members at a routine department meeting. Her violent and criminal past emerged after the event, sparking a debate whether this school shooting could have been prevented if the authorities acted sooner and recognized the signs of psychological problems she had since her twenties.

The shooting at the University of Alabama in Huntsville shocked the nation and the fact that the professor was the perpetrator proved that absolutely anyone can suffer a breakdown. Of course, there were countless problems that Amy Bishop had with her friends and co-workers at the university prior to this crime. But there were also some questionable details in her past which made the public certain that this wasn't her first murder.

Early life and education

Amy Bishop was born on April 24th in 1965 in Massachusetts. It was obvious from her early age that she was incredibly clever and gifted child. Amy loved science and wanted nothing more than to expand her knowledge and reach academic success. Her parents were highly educated and wanted to provide Amy with all possibilities to pursue her education. As a matter of fact, her father was an art professor at the well-known Northeastern University in Massachusetts.

Amy did end up enrolling into that same university and earned her bachelor's degree there. Of course, she wanted to go even further and accepted a challenge eagerly. She completed her Ph.D. at the Harvard University shortly after and her field of study was genetics. The very fact that her thesis was incredibly long and well researched will tell you a lot about her character and personality. Amy wasn't a quitter and had the need to be at the top of her class no matter what.

In the midst of her pursuit for knowledge, she managed to start a family and married James Anderson. Even though they had a turbulent relationship at first, they somehow made it work. The two of them have four children together. Amy's life seemed completely normal from the outside – she has a large and loving family, was interested in literature, and worked as a professor at a famous university. However, she wasn't a stranger to odd behavior and was often involved in unexplainable circumstances that did put her on the police's radar.

The first brush with the law

The first questionable event happened on the 8th of December 1986 when Amy was only 21 years old. She accidentally killed her younger brother with a shotgun. The whole accident does seem a bit strange right now but the inquiry into the shooting came to the conclusion that Amy didn't want to murder her brother and that the shotgun somehow misfired.

Apparently, the incident happened in the kitchen of the Bishop family house and Amy discharged the shotgun into her brother's chest. Their mother witnessed the entire event because she was in the same room and testified on Amy's behalf. On the other hand, the authorities did discover that Amy fired one shot into her bedroom wall prior to killing her brother. They did take a very close look at every single detail of this case but concluded that there was no intention behind this murder.

Amy was cleared of any suspicion but the event did not sit well with some of the officers working in Braintree at that time. The statements and files regarding the murder did disappear in 1988 but they were uncovered in 2010 leading to a brand new investigation even though the murder itself happened back in the 1980s. A couple of policemen that took on the case did come out publicly to say that the Braintree law enforcement was heavily corrupted back then and that Amy's mother had connections to people in charge. She insisted on meeting with the police chief at the time and Amy was set free a couple of hours later.

It is important to mention that Amy was in a relationship with her future husband back at the time of the murder but they were on a break. James returned to Amy shortly after and they rekindled their romance. He stood by her and believed in her innocence. The couple was soon married and moved on.

The accounts of the incident do vary and it is unknown why Amy shot her brother in the first place. It seems like it wasn't an accident due to the fact that a total of two shots were fired that night. Neighbors living near the Bishops did think that the brother and sister were arguing earlier that day but they couldn't provide the police with more details. It was later discovered that Amy fled the scene after shooting her brother and threatened two car dealership clerks with the same shotgun in order to attain a car, possibly to run away from the authorities. Amy did not suffer any consequences and continued to live her life as before but this crime will catch up with her.

The bomb in a letter

Amy Bishop's life continued to be hectic in the 1990s as well. But this time she had an accomplice – her husband. Paul Rosenberg worked with Bishop at the Children's Hospital at Boston and was her supervisor. In 1993 he received a package in the mail containing two homemade pipe bombs that didn't go off after he opened it. They were either broken or weren't assembled properly. Rosenberg called the police and they shortly narrowed down the list of suspects.

Amy Bishop loved her job at the Children's Hospital and was very concerned about the negative report she received from Paul Rosenberg. She was forced to resign from her position due to the fact that Rosenberg thought she wasn't a good fit for the hospital and that she lacked experience. After receiving her evaluation, Amy was visibly upset and showed signs of a possible mental breakdown in front of her co-workers.

Amy's psychological state had a huge influence on her husband as well and he was sure that Paul Rosenberg's evaluation was faulty. He became angry with Amy's supervisor and one witness who contacted the law enforcement once the investigation started said that James Anderson wanted to murder Paul Rosenberg because he fired his wife.

The police didn't have any solid evidence that could connect Amy Bishop and James Anderson directly to the pipe bombs. The spouses refused to let the detectives search their home in order to find any traces of explosives and they stopped talking and communicating with them as well.

The investigators were sure that Bishop and Anderson made the bombs but the lack of evidence left the murder attempt unsolved. This case will be revisited after the shooting at the University of Alabama but the investigators would not reach a definite conclusion. The judge confirmed that she was certain Amy Bishop and her husband were the ones who sent the package to Paul Rosenberg even though there were no physical traces anywhere on the bombs or package. They were the only ones who wanted to harm the doctor and had strong negative feelings toward him.

Anger management issues

The next incident that involved Amy Bishop happened in an International House of Pancakes. Even though it seems trivial, the attack was an evidence that Amy had a lot of unresolved psychological issues that were starting to come out to the surface. The inability to get the last booster seat led to a sudden burst of aggression towards another guest of the restaurant.

Bishop casually strolled to this woman's table and asked her to give her the booster seat. When the woman refused, Bishop swung her arm and hit the woman in her face screaming at the top of her lungs: "I am Dr. Amy Bishop!" The other guests who witnessed the incident were shocked by Bishop's behavior and called the authorities right away.

Amy Bishop ended up in the police station, accepting the full responsibility for the attack without showing any remorse for her violent behavior. She pleaded guilty and received probation. The attorneys who prosecuted her demanded that Bishop attends anger management classes but it seems like the judge ignored their demands. There were no records that Bishop ever attended any or received psychological help in order to deal with her issues.

Career at the University of Alabama

Amy Bishop and her husband continued to be heavily involved in the scientific community and they worked together on several projects. They invented the portable cell incubator which won a couple of awards and they moved on to perfecting their invention with some financial help from people interested in using their incubator in the near future.

Amy Bishop worked at Harvard Medical School before she relocated to the University of Alabama in Huntsville back in 2003. She applied for a position of an assistant teacher and got accepted. Her academic achievements spoke for themselves and the university though she would be a valuable addition to their biology department.

Other professors who worked closely with Bishop did testify that she was slightly strange and would often speak about topics unrelated to a discussion they were having at the moment. But it wasn't alarming at all. It fit her character because she was known to be slightly odd. Bishop didn't manage to fit in and she wasn't a favorite among students either. They would often complain that Bishop wasn't a good professor and was unable to share her knowledge with the rest of the class properly. It was clear that she was smart but Amy simply wasn't made to be a lecturer and it showed.

She lacked charisma, patience, communication skills, and the students would often leave her lectures completely confused. Science teachers often get very involved in their studies which might lead them to become antisocial and withdrawn from the rest of the society. Bishop could be very unpleasant to a class she was teaching and numerous students left the university because of her. The complaints continued to be filed for years but they didn't have any effect.

After six years at the University of Alabama, Amy Bishop was once again under review and the committee decided that they will terminate her contract, making the 2010 spring semester her last one at that institution. She tried to file a complaint to the tenure but the chances are she would be leaving the university very soon.

As you might have guessed, the news shocked Bishop and she probably started spinning out of control from the very moment she was told that they were letting her go. We could blame the tenure for this incident but it simply isn't enough. Bishop's personality that rarely accepted failure combined with the underlying aggression she carried inside made this seemingly normal woman to snap. After all, the position of a professor was something she worked her whole life for and there was no way she would go away so easily.

Amy managed to find out what led to the negative review and discovered that her colleagues were partly to blame. They told the committee that she was odd and slightly crazy, citing all the student complaints that kept piling in over the years. She decided to hit them back and contacted Equal Employment Opportunity Commission saying that her colleagues were discriminating her because of her gender. She was certain that the fact that she was a woman was the core of the problem. Bishop's colleagues stood by their statements and

Equal Employment Opportunity Commission couldn't find anything that would prove Bishop's claims of gender discrimination.

Amy Bishop's contract was supposed to end on 12th February but she would continue teaching at the university for a few more weeks. It was apparent that Amy's mental health was falling apart but her husband still stood by his wife's side and supported her fight to stay at this institution. February 12th, 2010 marks the date when the situation at the University of Alabama escalated and Amy Bishop opened fire on her colleagues at a routine faculty members meeting.

She waited patiently for her opportunity and there was no way she could allow the moment to get away for her. The date carries a lot of symbolism to her and it seems like she saw it as her personal vendetta against the other professors working at the same department. She felt betrayed by the team she closely collaborated with for years and the only way she could get her way was by murdering every single one of them.

The day of the shooting

On the 12th of February, everything was going smoothly at the university. Classes were being held and students attended lectures – there were no signs that anything could go wrong. Amy Bishop followed her schedule for the day as well, teaching two classes in the morning and around the noon. The students who were in her anatomy and neuroscience classes would later say that they didn't notice any changes in Bishop's behavior.

A standard faculty meeting was planned to start later in the afternoon. The professors working at the Biology and Mathematics departments slowly gathered in the Room 369 and occupied their seats. Everyone was there including Bishop. She listened to everything that was discussed at the meeting but kept to herself without speaking too much unless asked to do so. There were thirteen faculty members in the room.

Amy Bishop stood up in the middle of the meeting and pulled out a 9mm handgun. It would be later discovered that she didn't have a valid permission to carry any firearm with her. She apparently took the gun from her husband without his knowledge. Joseph Ng who worked as a fellow professor at the University of Alabama at Huntsville would later state: "Bishop got up suddenly, took out a gun and started shooting at each one of us. She started with the one closest to her, and went down the row shooting her targets in the head." Other witness described the killings as "execution style". It was clear that Bishop knew what she was doing and who she wanted dead.

But the unexpected thing happened right in the middle of the attack – her handgun either run out of bullets or got jammed. Bishop was pulling the trigger but the gun would only click. This prevented a larger catastrophe. This setback agitated Bishop and it was the perfect time for Joseph Ng to step in and try to keep her from attacking the rest of the faculty members. He carefully got closer to Bishop and other professors joined him. They managed to push Bishop through the door. She ended up in the hallway while her colleagues stayed in the meeting room. They started barricading themselves inside and called the local police.

Amy Bishop was arrested shortly after the shooting. Sheriff's deputy was one of the first responders and he approached her with confidence even though she could have been armed. The law enforcement found her standing in front of the Shelby Center for Science and Technology and she didn't try to run away or resist the arrest. As a matter of fact, she seemed to be completely unaware of the events that happened in the Room 369. The arresting police officers asked her why she killed her colleagues and she responded by saying that she didn't hurt anyone and that the faculty members were alive and well.

The law enforcement entered the building alongside the emergency personnel. They tended the wounded professors and took a closer look at the crime scene. The pistol which was used in the shooting was discovered in the bathroom. Amy Bishop probably placed it there before exiting the building in an attempt to distance herself from the weapon.

In the end, Amy Bishop murdered three of her colleagues and wounded three more. Gopi Podila was the head of the biology department and Bishop probably held a grudge against him the most. Maria Ragland Davis and Adriel D. Johnson Sr. were fellow biology professors working at the University of Alabama for years. It is a huge tragedy that could have been prevented if the authorities did their job properly decades ago. The fact that the gun stopped working in the middle of the killing spree probably saved many lives. It is important to mention that only a handful of students were actually in the building during the shooting and none of them were injured.

The survivors were afraid that Amy Bishop left a so-called herpes bomb in one of the classrooms on her floor because she had access to the virus. Her research did include this particular strain and she has a vast knowledge on the topic so it was a possibility. The police would end up combing each and every floor in order to make sure nobody gets hurt once they open up the building again. No such device was found on the university grounds.

Her husband was informed of the events and he seemed to be shocked. It looked like he was completely in the dark about Amy's plans to get revenge over the tenure. The police questioned him back at the station and in his interview he stated that Amy called him after the shooting, pleading that he comes to the university in order to pick her up. Apparently, he refused to do it but certainly looks like she was waiting for him in front of the building.

Interrogation and psychological problems

When the police officers who were in charge of the investigation started talking to Bishop, it was clear that the woman was slightly delusional. She would constantly repeat sentences such as: "I wasn't there. It wasn't me." The interrogation was almost impossible due to Bishop's reluctant answers but she did acknowledge what she had done at the University of Alabama in Huntsville.

When we take a closer look at Bishop's past, it is evident that there were a lot of underlying psychological problems that went untreated. Her colleagues often described her as odd and quirky but she could also be very defensive and confrontational. After the attack at the restaurant and the probation sentence, her aggression became pretty well known. Those suggested anger management classes probably could have helped her a bit but they wouldn't solve everything.

The fact that she very likely murdered her brother back in the 1980s after a family quarrel and that Bishop continued living her life as if nothing happened could be interpreted as a narcissistic behavior combined with sociopathy. She had a hard time accepting the defeat and would often resolve the problems by acting aggressively towards the person she thought was responsible for her downfall which can be seen in the way she treated her supervisor at the Children's Hospital.

The law enforcement investigated this case furthermore and searched Bishop's house in order to find any evidence to what led to the shooting at the university. They took away her personal computer, as well as any documentation related to her firing from the teaching position. Amy Bishop was charged with one count of capital murder. Three charges of attempted murder were also included. Bishop decided not to involve the family attorney in her case and choose a court-appointed lawyer. The sentencing would either be life in prison or death penalty. There was a possibility for a parole in case she ends up in a prison.

Roy W. Miller who was her lawyer visited Bishop in the prison and did his own psychological evaluation before the two of them went to the court. Miller later said to the media that Bishop has serious mental problems and that she is probably bordering on paranoid schizophrenia. He even went very far and called his client „a wacko".

Miller would quickly retract his statements and say that Bishop's mind wasn't fully there during the shooting but he does understand that his client is undoubtedly guilty of the crime. His exact statement was: "This is not a whodunit. This lady has committed this offense or offenses in front of the world. It gets to be a question in my mind of her mental capacity at the time or her mental state at the time that these acts were committed."

Sentencing

Amy Bishop was the first professor or a faculty member in the history of the US who opened fire at a school or a university and murdered their own colleagues. She was clearly guilty because numerous survivors witnessed the entire event first hand and they were absolutely sure that Amy Bishop was the cold-blooded murderer.

In the meantime, the police re-investigated the case involving the murder of Bishop's brother back in 1986. After they took a closer look at the collected the physical evidence and files which were presumably lost, Amy Bishop was indicted. They determined she killed her brother as well and that it wasn't an accident as it was claimed by her mother.

This didn't help with Bishop's mental state at all and the problems piled up. Her attorney did say that Amy was feeling very sorry for the shooting at the University of Alabama in Huntsville a couple of weeks earlier. On 18th of June, 2010 Bishop tried to commit suicide while incarcerated but was rescued by the guards. After a short stint at the hospital, Bishop was transferred back to her jail cell but the guards kept a close eye on her and her behavior.

The preliminary trial began in September of 2011 but the final sentencing would arrive one year later. Amy Bishop stood in front of a crowded courtroom and pleaded not guilty. Roy W. Miller decided to use the insanity defense after sending his own psychiatrist to examine Bishop in the prison.

On 24th of September 2012, Amy Bishop was sentenced to life in prison. She wouldn't be able to appeal the verdict. She was also found guilty in Massachusetts for killing her brother but she wouldn't go to trial for that. Bishop did insist that she wanted to tell her story in front of the judges but Massachusetts refused to allow it because Alabama did have more strict punishments and the people in charge thought that life in prison is quite enough.

Amy Bishop didn't want to give up her possibility of an appeal so she tried to make a judge grant her a new opportunity. She filed a complaint in 2013 saying that her verdict wasn't explained to her properly and that she didn't understand the consequences. Two months later, she got an answer from the judge and her possibility of appeal was rejected. It is clear that Amy Bishop will spend the rest of her life behind the bars.

She is currently serving her time at Julia Tutwiler Prison for Women which is located in Wetumpka, Alabama. She continued to be a burden and Bishop's behavior didn't improve at all. She was involved in a physical attack on Amy Maclin who is a fellow inmate, injuring the woman. Bishop suffered a couple of bruises herself after Maclin used a tray in order to defend herself from her attacker.

This only proves that Bishop has anger management issues and that the insanity plea was purely for show. Bishop if fully aware of her actions and many experts who were closely following this case are certain that she planned the shooting at the University of Alabama in Huntsville for at least a couple of weeks before the crime.

LETHAL LOVERS: THE TRUE STORY OF CATHERINE MAY WOOD

JESSI DIXON

Lethal lovers

"You're going to hear about love. You are going to hear about jealously. You are going to hear about hatred," lawyer James Piazza told the jury during Gwendolyn Graham's trial in November 1989. "You will hear, through the testimony, about revenge. All (can be found) in heterosexual relationships. The same emotions are going to play here before you in the next week."

During the course of the trial, the jury listened to the story of Graham and Catherine May Wood – young lesbian lovers who enhanced their sexual play by killing elderly patients at the nursing home where they worked. Together, the two women would smother their victims, and on more than one occasion, would make love while washing the bodies of their recently murdered patients.

Wood and Graham met shortly after Graham moved from Texas to Michigan, where she took a job working with Wood at the Alpine Manor. The two women became fast friends, then lovers, by 1986 - and only two years later, they had been charged with the murders of five elderly patients.

Marguerite Chambers, age 60; Myrtle Luce, age 95; Mae Mason, age 79; Belle Burkhard, age 74; and Edith Cook, age 97, all lost their lives at the hands of these lethal lovers.

Pain and pleasure

After the marriage she'd entered into as a teenager broke up after seven years, Wood took a job at Alpine Manor in July 1985 – and was quickly promoted to supervisor of nurses aides. Despite her success on the job, Wood was still having trouble making friends, and at 450 pounds, she felt self-conscious about her appearance.

However, once Graham started working at Alpine Manor directly under Wood, her social life began to pick up. Together, the women began visiting gay bars, going to parties, and enjoying rough casual sex. Wood even started dieting.

According to Wood, Graham had initially brought up premeditated murder in October 1986, but she thought it was just part of a sexual game. By January 1987, Graham's desires had become more specific, and she told Wood she was interested in killing a patient.

"We were at home in the bedroom and she said she wanted to kill somebody at the Manor, and I just – that was about it, I didn't pay much attention," Wood confessed at Graham's trial.

"I asked her how, and she said she wanted to do it – she was going to suffocate them, and I said something about, with a pillow, and she said no she – that they would turn their heads, so that she would use washcloths to hole their nose and then their mouth. And I had asked her why, and she says to keep – because she would have to apply so much pressure that they would have indentations or bruises from pushing."

Wood claimed that Graham was a very dominant lover – often tying her down during sex and choking her or smothering her with a pillow until she nearly passed out. Wood never complained about Graham's aggressive lovemaking, and she started to recognize the similarities between pain and pleasure.

"Just talking about murder got them both excited," said a TruTV report about the killings. "The linked pain and pleasure of their sexual games became threaded with the idea of cruelty."

In an article published in the Williamson Daily News on December 7, 1988, Police Chief Walt Sprenger admitted that the intimate relationship between the two women was "part of a complex web that brings the whole thing together."

Too far gone

Wood received reduced charges thanks to a plea bargain agreement - spilling to the police all the details of the murders and testifying against Graham in her trial. Although Wood portrayed Graham as the criminal mastermind, her claims were refuted in a book by award-winning journalist Lowell Cauffiel, *Forever and Five Days*.

Released in 1992, the book explores the murders and the "love bond" shared by the two women.

Wood's account describes the first murder as taking place in January of 1987, when Graham smothered a patient suffering from Alzheimer's disease with a washcloth while Wood acted as a lookout. Too ill to defend herself, the woman became the couple's first victim - and since the death appeared to be of natural causes, there was no need for an autopsy. According to Wood, Graham claimed to have murdered the patient to "relieve her tension."

This first murder did help solidify the bond between Wood and Graham, as each felt confident that sharing the secret of the murder meant the other woman wouldn't be able to leave the relationship. "We were supposed to take turns killing so we could never leave each other," Wood stated in her testimony at Graham's trial.

The couple also enjoyed their success together – Graham had attempted to murder at least two targets who had been able to defend themselves before finally selecting a victim too far gone to fight back. They began selecting victims by pinching their noses to see if they would struggle.

"She was always real happy afterwards and I wanted her to be happy," Wood said. "I never told her 'no.' ... I never loved anybody the way I loved her."

As the next few months passed, Wood claimed Graham killed another four patients at Alpine Manor - who all ranged in age from 65 to 97. The women all suffered from Alzheimer's disease and were, according to Wood, incapacitated. In her testimony, Wood alleged that she and Graham started a game to select their next victim - trying to choose initials to spell out M-U-R-D-E. That became too difficult, and the women started counting each kill as a "day," referring to the phrase "I will love you forever and a day." Also introduced at the trial was a poem Wood wrote for Graham, which ended with, "you'll be mine forever and five days."

"Sometimes, the sheer excitement of the killing was too much," described one account of the events, "and they retired immediately to an empty room for sex while memories were fresh."

On other occasions, the couple would relive the murders after the fact – using the mementos Wood claimed that Graham had taken from each victim. However, these souvenirs were never found by the police, despite the fact that some accounts show that at least three nurses claimed they saw the shelf of souvenirs at the home Graham and Wood shared. These reportedly included an anklet, handkerchief, brooch, or a set of dentures.

Graham was also presented as being dominant in her relationship with Wood - sexually, physically, and emotionally, according to Wood's testimony. Graham reportedly even encouraged Wood to take on a more active role in their game – and asked her to kill a victim of her own to prove her love. Since she was unable to go through with it, she was transferred to another shift.

"I didn't think it was right," Wood said. "A lot of those people had a lot of life left in them and we were there to care for them, not abuse them."

Eventually, the relationship came to an end when Graham started seeing Heather Barager, another female nursing aide who worked with them at Alpine Manor, and the pair moved to Texas. Graham started working at a hospital, caring for infants. Wood and Graham still kept in touch via telephone.

According to Wood, Graham's new position working with infants encouraged her to come clean about the couple's murderous past.

"When she was killing people at Alpine and I didn't do anything, that was bad enough," Wood told the court at Graham's trial. "But when she would call me and say how she wanted to smash a baby, I had to stop her somehow. I knew she was working in a hospital there. She said she wanted to take one of the babies and smash it up against a window. I had to do something. I didn't care about myself anymore."

And so, Wood told her ex-husband, Ken Wood, about the murders she'd been involved with.

"It was nothing."

Wood was born on an army base in Washington state in March, 1962. Upon his return from Vietnam, Wood's father suffered from PTSD and frequent night terrors – and would often become emotionally and mentally abusive toward his two young daughers. According to Wood's sister Barbara Burns, the girls became quite close as a result of growing up in a "dysfunctional family."

"Cathy was a bookworm, she was very smart," Burns said. "She would stay in her bedroom and read. I think she also did that because she was tall and heavy, and the other kids could be very cruel to her, because of her size."

Her father was particularly cruel, Wood said, noting that he made her "feel real ugly" when she was around 12 or 13 – just as she began noticing a growing attraction to boys. However, Wood's first sexual experience ended up being with a woman.

"David" dressed as a man, and according to Wood, used a strap-on dildo during their sexual interactions. At first, Wood claims she didn't even know he was a woman.

One day, Wood placed a phone call to her friend Terry, which was received by his older brother Ken. She and Ken wound up chatting on the phone for five hours before she agreed to go out on a date with him – and, because of her experience with David, Wood slept with him on their first date just to be sure that he was actually a man.

However, Wood found their relationship unsatisfying – particularly sexually.

"I didn't like him touching me and I didn't like spending any time with him," Wood said. "Sex was just… it was nothing. Something you had to do, something you did because your husband wanted to. It wasn't fun, it wasn't interesting. He just did it and then went and watched football."

The couple married when Wood was only sixteen years old and pregnant. By all accounts, Wood was miserable in her marriage – she was depressed, overweight, neglected her housekeeping, and displayed little affection toward her daughter. Her relationship with Ken suffered, and the couple separated briefly in 1984 before attempting a reconciliation with the help of a marriage counselor.

As a teenager, Wood had worked as a candy striper at the hospital – and when she needed to find a job after finally leaving her husband in 1985, she decided to look into an open position at a nursing home called Alpine Manor to use some of the skills she'd developed. Shortly after she started working at the home, Wood said a coworker named Dawn started showing her attention – and, after her past experience with David, she started to question her sexuality.

But only three weeks into her new lesbian relationship with Dawn, Wood started spending more time with Graham – and only three weeks after that, the two moved in together. Initially, according to Wood, they were just going to be roommates, but she said that arrangement lasted "maybe five minutes" before they became lovers.

Wood said the relationship was satisfying, though, because she and Graham were "equals." They were a team who made decisions together – and with Graham, she said she learned that sex could be "nice."

"When Cathy met Gwen, it was the first time in her life that she ever sowed her oats," Burns said. "She'd been a stay-at-home person growing up, and when she got married to Ken, she never left the house. So when she separated from Ken and met Gwen, she started going out to movies, playing pool, started living for the first time in her life. But over time, she changed – she became hard."

A criminal mastermind

Still, Wood's confession to Ken about the murders wasn't the first time she had told her ex-husband something grisly – she'd confided in him years ago that she'd always been curious about what it would feel like to stab another person. Ken stalled for fourteen months before finally telling the police.

"I thought about the families of the victims; so many people were going to get hurt," said Ken, adding that he had promised his ex-wife that he wouldn't tell anyone. "But Cathy wasn't getting any better. I sensed a lot of guilt. She couldn't let go of what had happened ... I went to the police because she needed help."

An investigation began shortly, with Wood questioned extensively by the Walker Police Department's detectives. Slowly, she began to describe her version of the killings, pinning the majority of the blame on Graham.

"She would give tidbits, small information that led me to believe that she might possibly be involved in the actual killings," said Lieutenant Tom Freeman with the Walker Police Department. "At the same time, as an investigator, I had nothing to go on – only her testimony."

Two of the couple's victims were exhumed, as they had not been cremated, but a medical examination still revealed no physical evidence of foul play. According to Dr. Stephen Cohle, who examined the bodies of victims Marguerite Chambers and Edith Cook, cause of death could not be established based on the examination alone.

"There was no pathological evidence of suffocation," Cohle reportedly told the court. "However, there also was no overwhelming pathological evidence that natural conditions had caused their deaths."

Chambers' death certificate indicated that she died of a heart attack, which Cohle ruled out on his examination. While Chambers did have Alzheimer's disease, he stated she "could have lived perhaps several months, or possibly years longer." Cook's examination revealed narrowing in her coronary arteries, but Cohle noted that this was not severe enough to have been life-threatening.

"It's not that she couldn't have died of it, but it isn't very likely," he said. "(Police) don't go around looking for homicides where there is no evidence of homicide. I basically felt that the statements (made by Wood) were valid."

Since inconclusive results like this are consistent with many smothering cases, the deaths were still ruled as homicides by the medical examiner based on the information Wood had revealed to police. After warrants were issues for Wood and Graham's arrests, the women were brought in and charged with two murders in December of 1988.

"It is a case in which practically no physical evidence exists to prove a crime was committed," read an article published in the September 11, 1989 edition of the Argus-Press. "It appears to be based almost entirely on confessions from Graham's alleged accomplice and former lover, Catherine Wood."

During the trial, Wood continued to portray Graham as the criminal mastermind, claiming that Graham planned and committed each murder while Wood simply acted as a lookout. She was able to successfully plea-bargain down to a reduced sentence, and continued to maintain her innocence. Although there was no evidence to support Wood's allegations, Graham's new girlfriend did testify that Graham had confessed that she'd killed five patients - and the jury was convinced.

"Without you, I'm sure this matter never would have been cleared up," said Circuit Judge Robert Benson to Wood.

Graham received five life sentences from the court in November 1989, after she was found guilty of five counts of murder and one count of conspiracy to commit murder. She is currently serving her time in the Women's Huron Valley Correctional Facility in Michigan.

As for Wood, she received 20 years each on one count of second-degree murder and one count of conspiracy to commit second-degree murder. While she has been eligible for parole since March of 2005, Wood remains incarcerated in Federal Correctional Institution, a minimum security facility in Florida. Wood has been denied parole seven times, but her release is currently scheduled for June 6, 2021.

A "coercive and seductive pathological liar"

"There are two Cathy Woods, really. One of them wears a mask of sanity, and that mask portrays a relatively quiet, intelligent, articulate individual who seems at first, rather likeable and rather passive – not very aggressive at all," said Lowell Cauffiel. "But behind that mask is a cunning, manipulative psychopath."

Lowell Cauffiel's book, *Forever and Five Days*, depicts a dramatically different scenario. The non-fiction narrative explains how friends, family members, and coworkers who knew Wood and Graham said Wood was a "coercive and seductive pathological liar who delighted in wreaking havoc in the lives of others."

Tony Kubiak, who worked at Alpine Manor with both Wood and Graham, said that when he found out the facility was under investigation and that the police had identified two potential suspects, he surmised it may have something to do with Wood and someone else – possibly Graham.

"She's evil enough to kill," he said. "It wasn't (Graham) and somebody – it was (Wood) and somebody."

While Kubiak admitted Graham was likely the more violent of the two, Wood was the dominant one. Twice as big as Graham, and he had seen her pull Graham into a bedroom by her hair. He recalled Wood setting up pranks and revenge schemes while working at the home – she'd even threatened that he was on her "revenge list."

"She's insane," he said. "Cathy Wood is sick in the head."

In his book, Cauffiel offers compelling evidence to support a theory that Wood, in fact, planned that first murder as a way to guarantee Graham would never leave her - insurance she felt she needed after catching her lover with another woman.

"She tied me up to the bed, and she put a gun in between my legs … and I was begging, because I thought she was going to shoot me,"

Graham said. "She just stood there for a minute, with it in me, and then she took it out and looked at me real strange, and then she left the house."

When even the secret of the murders wasn't enough to keep Graham from leaving her, Wood took the story to police - putting herself in legal jeopardy in order to seek revenge against her ex-lover. *Forever and Five Days* reveals a darker, more psychotic side to Wood, portraying her as the criminal mastermind who not only manipulated Graham into executing a series of murders but also manipulated the court to buy into her fabricated account.

According to Cauffiel's book, psychological testing done on Graham helped support the theory - as a sufferer of borderline personality disorder, Graham would be easy to manipulate. She also couldn't have been able to plan the sophisticated series of murders, or effectively defend herself during the trial.

"Gwen Graham is very mixed-up woman who comes out of a childhood involving a certain amount of abuse. (She's) a very dependent individual, a person eager to please the partner that she's with – somewhat of a tragic figure, actually," Cauffiel said.

The size difference between the two women also stuck with several witnesses and audience members of the trials. The granddaughter of Mae Mason, one of the couple's victims, watched as Wood sobbed through her questioning during the trial.

"It just astounded me that a three-hundred-pound woman could feel so afraid of Gwen Graham," said eighteen-year-old Stephanie Engman. "She was *too* sorry for what she had done."

Inmates who were incarcerated with Wood also reveal in the book that she told them two versions of the story that did not support the version she told police. In the first, she claimed to have invented the entire story to punish Graham for leaving her, and in the second, she confessed that she'd committed all the murders - but, to exact her revenge, she'd framed Graham for it.

"Yeah, I did it," inmate Margaret Mann remembered Wood saying. "Gwen was the lookout. Gwen watched my back."

In her testimony, Graham fervently denied the accusations that she had smothered patients – and even claimed that she didn't know of any murders that had even occurred at the home. In fact, Graham alleged that Wood frequently concocted rumors that she would spread around the nursing home, and Graham only went along with them to humor Wood.

"I was not present at the time of any of these people's deaths," Graham said. "I was somewhere in the building, working. That's all I know."

The murder plot, she said, was one Wood's "head games," just a joke. Until Graham started seeing another woman, and Wood began threatening to take the story to the police. Eventually, when she realized the police had been investigating the deaths, Graham concluded that Wood "was going to get even, just like she said she was."

"She wanted to know If it was true, and if it was true, she wasn't going to take the whole blame for (the slayings)," said Baragar in her testimony at Graham's trial. "Cathy was a part of it."

Graham also refuted the testimonies of some of her friends and former lovers, who claimed that Graham had confessed to smothering patients – but Graham said she'd only been relating to them the fabricated story Wood had come up with. According to an article from the September 19, 1989 edition of the Argus-Press, Graham was "visibly shaken" as Baragar recounted her "confessions."

Her decision to leave Wood and move to Texas with Barager, Graham said, was because she'd gotten "tired of playing games, hurting people ... The games just got out of hand."

Her lawyer, James Piazza, did make a request that the charges against Graham be reduced or dismissed entirely, due to a lack of evidence. When the motion was denied by Judge Roman Snow, Piazza closed his argument by saying that the murder spree was entirely concocted by a vindictive Wood, who was looking to get even with her ex-lover by any means necessary.

"Gwen Graham is living in a horror right now because of the bizarre imagination of Cathy Wood," he said. "Just because (Wood) pleaded guilty doesn't mean Gwen Graham is guilty of anything – other than going along with bad jokes."

However, the jury accepted Wood's account of the events. According to jury foreman Glenn Russell, "we felt it was a story that nobody could just think up."

"Sometimes, I would like to say I just made it up," Wood said. "That would be so easy. And then everybody could just go back to being happy again, I guess. But that's not so."

Facing the fallout

"I had always been pleased with Alpine," said Linda Engman, daughter of victim Mae Mason. "I remember that phone call from the nursing home like it was yesterday. I was flabbergasted."

Alpine Manor was faced with lawsuits from several of the families of the victims, claiming they had hired "dangerous and unbalanced employees." According to a spokeswoman for the nursing home, Ginny Seyferth, counseling was provided to employees following the arrests – as police began investigating eight "suspicious" deaths that occurred between January to April 1987.

"Alpine Manor is devastated, but relieved that something is being done," Seyferth told news reporters in December 1988. "Both had very good reviews. Both were well-liked by the patients."

Alpine Manor has since shut down. The building is now home to a new nursing home, Sanctuary at Saint Mary's.

Ken is still struggling to come to terms with his ex-wife's actions – and the burden that places on their daughter.

"Am I going to be able to give my child a normal upbringing, with her knowing who her mother is?" Ken said. "She can't hide that fact. That's what angers me."

Wood, who remains incarcerated, attempted to illegally solicit a penpal in 2013 by posting an ad on an online dating site. While inmates in Florida are welcome to receive mail from pen pals, they are strictly prohibited from seeking them out.

"Teach me! I've been incarcerated for two decades," Wood's profile stated. "I go to the parole board soon and I need someone who's kind and patient to teach me about the exciting new things in the world. I'm looking for a friend, male or female, to teach me everything I forgot. Are you honest? I am honest and non-judgmental. We can talk about anything and everything. I've never done drugs and I don't smoke. I like to play and have fun. Do you have time for a good friend?"

Graham, on the other hand, still maintains her innocence – claiming even years later that the entire story was fabricated by Wood to punish her for leaving.

"I'm innocent," Graham said. "I can no more prove that I'm innocent than they ever proved that I was guilty. I'm stuck here because of her word."

According to Ken Kolker with the Grand Rapids Press, we may never know what really happened with the Alpine Manor murders.

"When you look into different cases, you almost always get this gut feeling that either they did it or they didn't do it," he said. "And this is one of those cases where you gut feeling is that I don't know if it even happened – and if it happened, I don't know who was running the show."

JAMILA : SLUT & KILLER

JANET BROWNRIDGE

She was rumored to be the prostitute lover of such celebrities as George Clooney and Bruce Willis. But in 2004, Jamila M'Barek would make headlines of her own.

Her name would be thrust into the spotlight when her sixty-four-year-old lover, Anthony Ashley-Cooper, the 10th Earl of Shaftsbury went missing. Five months later, he would found dead within a deep ravine at the foot of the French Alps, his horribly decomposed body half-eaten by wild animals.

Fingers of blame soon pointed to two unlikely suspects.

The exotic and beautiful Tunisian escort, Jamila M'Barek and her stoic brother, Muhammad M'Barek. The question was, what singular thread linked a rich, playboy aristocrat, a psychopathic petty criminal and a prostitute from the French Riviera?

The answer – one had a lust for money, the other had a lust for sex...

EARLY LIFE

Jamila M'Barek was born in 1961 in the storied and tiny northern commune of Lens, Pas de Calais in France. Despite the beautiful and seemingly idyllic surroundings, young Jamila's life was anything but peaceful due to the temper tantrums of her father, a violent binge drinking alcoholic. To escape her miserable homelife, Jamila and her six siblings (the eighth died at seven months of age) ran away from the home with her mother. The matriarch of the family brought them to the Arabic speaking Republic of Tunisia in Northern Africa after securing a divorce.

Free from her abusive father, the family felt security for the first time. But this was but a momentary illusion, for they could only afford to live in the most unsavory of slums and were readily ostracized due to the fact that divorce is considered wholly taboo by popular Tunisian society.

"Our neighbors rejected us because they saw us as foreigners," Jamila's sister Fatima said. "Because they knew how bad of a man our father was, and most of all because my parents were divorced."

"This ostracization made an indelible imprint on Jamila's mind," forensic psychologist Paula Orange said. "She hated the fact that her family was looked down upon. She would be willing to do whatever it took to not only gain power but influence. In the years ahead, this would mean using her body."

Jamila was determined to get ahead. She had a great deal of intellectual savvy and graduated near the top of her class.

"Jamila is very intelligent, always was," Fatima said. "She was always in the top two in her class and at the end of the school year, she received a prize, [every year] without fail. She was our role model. We always wanted to be like Jamila."

The adoration Jamila received from her family, however, would not last for very long. When she was only seventeen, Jamila moved to the former military stronghold town of Sant-Troupès, where she fell into a torrid relationship with a rich businessman from the Netherlands named Raf Schouten. Jamila became pregnant and bore Schouten both a son, named Raf in honor of the father, and a daughter, Kiara, and for a time the marriage was a happy one.

But Jamila wanted more money than even the rich Raf was giving her. Inexplicably, the rich man's wife turned to prostitution.

"It is a head scratcher," Orange said. "Until you take into account the trauma Jamila experienced in her upbringing. Money in and of itself would not be able to fill that psychological wound she experienced from being treated like a third-class citizen. Neither did having children. What she wanted was validation in the eyes of the world. A status that she could acquire. Prostitution gave her a sort of status as she would be wooed by high-status clientele."

Raf soon learned of Jamila's sordid nightly escapades, feeling shock and repulsion. He tried to talk her out of it but she only increased her activity.

"Jamila was equally as sick as all of her lovers," Orange said. "She could enjoy sex only when she was getting paid for it. That in and of itself was a peculiar fetish for her."

Raf could not handle the infidelity. He filed for a divorce.

Free from marital restraints and motherhood duties, Jamila plunged ahead with her hedonistic lifestyle. Word spread of the sexy North African with the great breasts and legs...not to mention her skills in the bedroom. Rumors of her sexual prowess would reach Hollywood circles. Word of her beauty eventually reached the heads of Playboy Magazine who solicited her for a nude photo shoot.

Jamila posed for the magazine in 1993 and the exposure allowed her to climb the social ladder while entering into an elite female escort service. She would be catering to a very specific and wealthy clientele, many of whom were rumored to have been foreign dignitaries and Hollywood playboys (including such celebrities as George Clooney and Bruce Willis).

THE BARON

Not long after joining this escort agency Jamila would meet the man who would change her life forever.

In the intermittent time between her first marriage and her second, Jamila retained a great deal of her wealth, owning two properties in affluent communities, one in Tunisia, the other in Cannes, France. She favored flashy, expensive clothing and lived the high life, making thousands of dollars per night.

"Jamila had a weird attraction to older men," Orange said. "She made it clear to her agency that she preferred them older and of course, rich."

The agency would oblige her when the Baron came into the city. He had heard of Jamila's reputation and wanted very much to meet her. After the agency hinted at how much money he had, she almost bolted out of the door to meet the mysterious older man who was awaiting her in Versailles.

En route, however, she found herself caught in a rain storm, the gusty weather mussing up her hair and clothes. Arriving at her destination, she realized who the palatial estate belonged to.

Anthony Tony Ashley-Cooper, the 10th Earl of Shaftsbury, Baron of Wimborne St. Giles and Baron of Pawlett, a descendant to one of the most recognized noble families in all of Britain.

"The Baron or The Duke, whatever you want to call him," Orange said. "Was the stereotypical bored rich guy. He moved to Paris where he didn't do anything but drink all day and have sex with high-end prostitutes."

Jamila arrived at his palace door, rain-soaked and looking like a mess. But the Baron paid her appearance no mind.

Upon her entrance, the Baron ushered Jamila into his foyer with a flurry of apologies, saying that it was all his fault that she had to weather such deplorable conditions.

The Baron was old but well-dressed, at least for what his role was on the French Riviera and that was of a well-to-do solicitor of prostitutes. He wore black leather pants, pink silk shirts and alligator skin shoes. This would all be topped off by a gold chain around his neck.

To Jamila's surprise, her first meeting with the Baron would be completely platonic.

"The Baron was content to just talk about himself," Orange said. "He talked about his family, his antiques, his paintings."

He ordered some pizza and gave Jamila some wine as they chatted away.

Jamila would fall asleep within a few hours, worn out by alcohol and the long-winded nature of the Baron's personality. But the Baron would wake her up early in the morning and their conversation continued.

After this initial date, a relationship quickly blossomed between them, one which was not entirely driven by the prospect of either sex nor payment. The Baron came across as a perfect client, he was harmless and fun. He did have one peculiar idiosyncrasy, as during the sex sessions with Jamila he would inexplicably shout out "Oh Mommy!"

Jamila, however, didn't care. The old man could call her whatever he wanted as long as she was paid and taken care of.

"They both had their own Oedipal complexes," Orange said. "The Baron obsessed on his mother. He had lost his grip on reality after she died." "You remind me of my mom," he would tell all of his lovers.

After sex, the Baron would ask his prostitute lover to read to him from a chapter in a book. His favorite? The biography of Napoleon.

"Of course, Jamila had her own Oedipal complex going on," Orange said. "She only got turned on by older men. She had to fill that hole left by her abusive father. She found a Daddy replacement in the Baron."

A LONG-TERM DEAL

Their relationship continued over the next few months until Jamila informed the Baron that she was pregnant.

"I don't want him to be a bastard," she said, reminding him of her own troubles as the product of a divorce.

"She put the Baron on the spot," Orange said. "He had no intentions of every marrying and his entire life was one of debauchery. His family got word of what happened and vehemently warned him against marrying the gold-digging prostitute from North Africa."

He didn't listen and the two would marry in a small but extravagant ceremony in the Netherlands.

The Baron would dote on his bride, showering her with gifts such as a custom-made windmill placed upon a lavish villa. He hired a staff of attendees and gave her a spending allotment of $100,000 per month.

"Orange made the mistake that most rich men make," Orange said. "Number one, he had no idea he was being played and wrote Jamila into his will."

Upon his death, Jamila would gain four million Euros as well as two pieces of high-end real estate in Nice.

VALIDATION

With the marriage to royalty, Jamila finally acquired the status she always craved. Or so she thought.

She began touting her title of "Countess" and was absolutely overjoyed to discover that she had her own street. Becoming instantly infatuated with her newfound status as literal royalty, Jamila shortly demanded her husband to take her to his ancestral home in St. Giles House in Dorset, a request which the kindly Earl readily obliged. However, the welcome she would receive would not be a warm one. When the Jamila opened the door, the couple was greeted by an elderly English housekeeper, or rather, the Baron was greeted, while Jamila was coldly ignored. This trend would continue through the exploration of the creaky manor until it reached such a point that the new Countess became quite flustered. However, she reached her breaking point when she was informed by one of Shaftsbury's son's that the house was reserved for the family heir, not the family heiress. Utterly indignant at her poor treatment and a figurative slap in the face, Jamila left in a rental car.

"It was a groundhog day moment for Jamila," Orange said. "She was disrespected yet again and it brought back memories of her days in Tunisia where she was invisible to everyone around her. She thought she had acquired the status she had longed for her whole life. Instead, she was treated like a nothing."

Jamila would never visit the old manor again.

A BUYER'S REMORSE

The Earl began having anxiety about his upcoming fatherhood. Would the child cramp his style? Would Jamila lose her tight body with the pregnancy? Thoughts like that raged through his head until one day he realized that Jamila looked the same. In fact, as she lounged around the pool area she looked as fit and firm as ever.

The Earl began to worry, it had been seven months since the wedding! Where was the baby bump?

Jamila assured her confused husband that she was simply the kind of woman upon whom pregnancy just did not show. The Earl was far from convinced and now the relationship began to take a turn for the worse.

"They began fighting," Orange said. "Ironically, their relationship had been a congenial one until the day the Baron had brought her to the manor. But now they began to fight. He had that feeling that her pregnancy was part of a ruse. A ruse to get money out of him."

Jamila would tell him that she had gotten an abortion. She further insulted him by saying that she would never have a child with a man who was a drug addict, alcoholic, sex pervert who called his lovers "mother" before his orgasms.

The Baron became furious, now realizing that his suspicions were spot on.

"He tried to kick her out of the house," Orange said. "She fought back. That is the amazing part. She thought she was entitled to whatever he had given her. That somehow it was her right to be called a 'Countess.'"

The Baron had given her something she didn't have before.

Status.

She had money with Raf but was still nothing more than his wife. But with the Baron, she was not merely the wife of a rich man, she was the wife of a noble – a descendant of British royalty. So alluring and seductive was this idea to Jamila that she would regularly wear a tiara out into public and curtly demand that all passersby refer to her as Countess or, Lady Shaftesbury. Naturally, this was not something Jamila wanted to lose.

"She begged, pleaded and threatened," Orange said. "But the Baron had made up his mind. He felt betrayed and no longer trusted the prostitute he pulled off the clubs of Versailles. She had to go."

PUBLIC HUMILIATION

Jamila then began attacking the Baron publicly, telling the newspapers of her husband's sexual perversions. She then returned to her previous life of a prostitute.

Jamila hosted lavish orgies at the Cannes flat which the Earl had gifted to her on their wedding day, one would be hard-pressed to find a more stark and venomous repudiation of a former lover. However, Jamila did maintain a small modicum of modesty, for when she began placing ads in the local newspapers for her prostitution agency she purposefully omitted the fact that she was a true Countess, deeming such a declaration to be indiscreet.

For well over a year the Earl of Shaftesbury ignored these libidinous affronts to his image, seemingly unconcerned. It appeared as if he had put Jamila completely out of his mind, that was until he met yet another stunning beauty named Nadia. Much in keeping with his passionate nature, the Earl had fallen completely head over heels for this new paramour and sought her hand in marriage.

But Jamila would not take kindly to her replacement.

Shortly after meeting Nadia, the Earl telephoned his former lover and informed her that he wanted a divorce.

Jamila responded only by saying, "You will be sorry."

Six months passed before the Earl took action, all the while Jamila continued to engage in prostitution, consorting with lecherous high-rollers and shadowy foreign dignitaries. On the fourth of November in 2004, the Earl drove took a long drive to the outskirts of Italy to garner the advice of fortune teller, a move that was much in keeping with his idiosyncratic character. He then spent a sleepless night carousing about the town before departing for the Noga Hilton of Cannes.

The next morning, Jamila received a phone call from the Earl. It was the day of their wedding anniversary and tensions were high. The Earl asked his former paramour to meet him for an early lunch to discuss the terms of their divorce. Jamila readily agreed but never showed up, leaving the Earl quite irate. He called again, perplexed and was told to meet Jamila at her apartment where they could discuss the issue in private. Thus, unshaven and groggy headed, the old adventurous aristocrat made the small pilgrimage to his former wife's apartment that sat along the storied Avenue Marechal Koenig. After making his way over the hill before the abode and through the huge, double gated entrance way, Tony Ashley-Copper, the 10th Earl of Shaftesbury was never to be seen alive again.

MURDER OF ROYALTY

The Earl entered the apartment and was given the cold shoulder by Jamila. Inside, he saw Jamila's brother, Muhammad M'barek. Muhammad was a former professional rugby player turned petty criminal. He was small but rugged and was described by all who knew him as a "money hungry psychopath."

Little did the Baron know that Jamila had hired her brother to kill him.

Her reasoning was that the Baron would file for divorce and her assets and inheritance, as well as her lauded title, would be irrevocably stripped from her in one single, fell swoop.

An argument quickly erupted and ended with Muhammad attacking the Earl. The older man was slammed to the floor and was no much for the vicious younger man. Muhammad squeezed the Baron's throat so forcibly that he snapped the Earl's neck, killing him instantly.

The brother and sister murder team threw the old man's body into their car. They drove to the base of the French Alps and tossed his body into a deep ravine.

For six months, not a single soul heard any word of the whereabouts of the Earl. However, the silence was broken during the ensuing police investigation with Jamila initially claiming that if anyone had killed her husband it was the youthful beauty, Nadia, the Earl's newest and last love. However, this theory didn't hold water, for

Nadia stood to gain nothing from the Earl's demise, as she was not written into his will.

What was clear was that Jamila stood to gain millions.

The police came next for her brother, Muhammad, at his residence at Munich. Muhammad, unsurprisingly, corroborated his sister's tale, saying that a fight did indeed break out between himself and the Earl, but that the old man's death had been but a tragic accident, a cruel twist of the fates. As the evidence mounted, the murderous duo's confidence began to crumble, slowly eroding away, bit by bit, piece by piece like the sonorous waves of the ocean slow-rending some ancient shale cliff-face.

Eventually, Jamila broke down in a hysterical fit and declared that she could no longer hide the truth, that her brother had indeed killed the Earl in a fight, but with the peculiar caveat that it had all just been a terrible accident. This did not fly either, for phone records show very clearly that it was nothing short of cold-blooded murder. The judge considered the case for but two scant hours before coming to a verdict.

Guilty on all counts.

After the terse hearing, both Jamila and her brother Muhammad were sentenced to twenty-five years of imprisonment, and for many years no word was heard from either of them.

Jamila, in particular, utterly refused any and all solicitations for interviews from the media and independent journalists and researchers alike. All the while maintaining her innocence and never expressing even the slightest shred of regret or remorse – in her mind, it was all just one terrible accident, a poor joke, an unforeseen twist of fate.

To this day she remains imprisoned and demands that the inmates and prison guards refer to her by the title she legally retains, "Countess Jamila M'Barek."

KILLER BABE : THE TRUE STORY OF BRITTANY
HOLBERG
JANET NIXON

Brittany Holberg was a twenty-three years old prostitute when she was convicted of murdering 80-year-old A.B. Towery Jr, stabbing him over sixty times.

The controversy surrounding the case centered around the relationship of Brittany and Towery prior to the killing. Brittany argued that Towery was a client who went into a rage when he found drugs on her person. He attacked her and she retaliated in self-defense.

Further investigation would reveal otherwise, however, as Brittany would use numerous household items in a brutal assault on the elderly man.

She fled the scene only to be caught at a McDonald's after police received a tip from a witness who saw her on "America's Most Wanted."

With her good looks and well-proportioned body, Brittany has remained in the spotlight as she was featured in a Maxim Magazine article as one of the "hottest women on death row".

Brittany still sits on death row today with her case being appealed on the numerous levels in the court system.

EARLY LIFE

Brittany was born on January 1, 1973, in Amarillo, Texas.

Accounts on Brittany's home life vary as she would manipulate according to the needs of her listener. To her probation officer, she informed them that her home life was "good" and that she "had everything that she ever wanted". She would often describe her mother as her best friend.

During other occasions, however, Brittany would paint a different story.

She would describe her parents as being "hippie-drugsters". Brittany would state that she was close to her mother but never knew her father, a heroin addict who was in and out of the Texas prison system. Her mother would later marry a man named John Schwartz with the couple marrying and divorcing four times.

They would drink heavily and openly smoke weed in front of the young Brittany who would be sexually assaulted by a babysitter at the age of five. When she was twelve, one of her aunts was murdered and according to Brittany "everything fell apart" at home. Her parents would leave her unattended as they indulged in pot and booze.

"They just stopped working," Brittany said. "They just let everything go."

She would be gang raped by two men who confronted her in an alley behind her home when she was thirteen.

Brittany would then spend the majority of her time living with her grandmother. By the age of sixteen, however, she would run away with her boyfriend Ward. The two would make it as far as California, get married, and have a young daughter named Mackenzie.

The union would not last long, however. Brittany would divorce Ward and move back to her native Amarillo. Ward would take Mackenzie and move to Tulsa, Oklahoma.

Brittany would state that she suffered a knee injury and would become addicted to pain medication during treatment. She would then graduate to harder drugs like cocaine.

In and out of rehab, Brittany's life spiraled out of control. She could manipulate with the best of them, however, and would escape from the Midland Halfway House with the help of a female counselor.

Brittany would hang out with the drug-using crowd and her own habits were out of control. To support her addiction, Brittany began working as a prostitute.

This would put her in harm's way on many an occasion as she would get gang-raped and beaten severely.

The assault would put her in the hospital but she would resume "tricking" when she was released.

"At that point in her life, Brittany was incorrigible," forensic psychologist Paula Orange said."Numerous people had reached to her and tried to help. She had extended family members trying to help. Friends trying to help. Even church outreach workers. All to no avail. The drugs had taken root and she was dead set on manipulating everyone around her. Family, roommates, church members, doctors, dentists, and pharmacists would all fall victim to her schemes to get drugs."

By 1993, Brittany was a full-blown drug-addicted prostitute with the rap sheet to prove it. In April of that year, she would steal a gun from her step-father. She then passed over $1300 in "hot" checks and applied for several store credit cards using a fake name.

Brittany and one of her aunts would run a scam on dentists, lying to them about their pain levels in order to get prescription medication. When the prescription drugs ran out, she would return to street drugs like cocaine and heroin. Arrests would follow and Brittany would be charged in Hale County with drug possession, paraphernalia, and public intoxication.

Upon her release, Brittany would proceed to steal her mother's car and forge checks in her name. The prostitution continued unabated as well as she stole the wallet from one of her "tricks" who pressed charges.

While in jail for the theft, Brittany would be introduced to Ella Gibbs and Patricia Karnes who ran the ministry in the Randall County Jail. The women tried to get Brittany on the right track and introduce her to Christianity.

"I wanted to reassure Brittany that she is a valuable person, that her life has great potential, and that this is the mortal portion of an eternal life," Karnes said. " Brittany is an eternal being and through the many prayers from my [prayer] group [in Lubbock,] I have been led to come back into this child's life to support her here, to encourage her, to find her courage from the Holy Spirit within her, and to let her know that there is a human being mortal person who will stand beside her and see the good in her and support whatever God plans for the rest of your [sic] life."

A.B. TOWERY

Towery was by all accounts a nice man. His son would bristle at the idea that he was Brittany's "sugar daddy".

"Dad wasn't a dirty old man," his son said. "Dad was just trying to help somebody and look what he got, and now she's getting three meals a day and a warm place to sleep."

The defense would later bring up the fact that he once pulled a knife on his son Russell during a temper tantrum. Towery would have a history with prostitutes (according to court testimony). Connie Baker would be a prostitute from the 1980s to 1997 and stated that Towery was one of her clients. Baker would also claim Tower as a client but she also had a history of drug possession and auto theft. Diana Wheeler would also admit to being one of Towery's prostitutes in the years of 1994 and 1995. She had come to his home and he even went so far as to clean the stains off his Mel Mac dinnerware. But Wheeler also had a long criminal history like Baker, arrested for prostitution, criminal trespass and giving false identification to a police officer.

The controversy at the trial was if Brittany and Towery had an ongoing "sex-for-money" relationship.

This would be vigorously discounted by family members.

His daughter-in-law would come to the home and help with some housekeeping. His sons would also visit daily and never report any "ladies of the evening" coming to visit their father.

The picture just didn't fit.

Brittany stated she was sent to Towery's place by a fellow streetwalker who went by the moniker of "Green Eyes" but that it was later revealed that no such prostitute by that name existed. Brittany had lied like she had so many times before.

The two seemed to have met by chance.

COMING BACK FROM THE GROCERY STORE

November 13th, 1996 was another normal day for the 80-year old A.B Towery. He had just purchased groceries at an Albertson's store and was walking back to his apartment. As he entered the courtyard, he was approached by the 23-year old Brittany Holberg.

She asked to use his telephone and Towery consented. He wanted to help the sweet-voiced Brittany and didn't believe that she posed any kind of physical threat to him.

What he didn't know was that Brittany was coming down from a cocaine high and had not slept in ten days.

"Brittany could be persuasive," Orange said. "She was well-versed in how to charm people, she knew exactly what to say and do in terms of body language. She was like a trained actress. It didn't take much cajoling on her part to convince Towery to let her inside his home. He probably thought 'what's the big deal?'"

Once inside, Brittany would demand money from the elderly man but he refused. Brittany then attacked Towery, trying to strong arm the wallet out of his pocket. The struggle began in the living room. The two then pushed and pulled each other around a partition that separated the kitchen from the living room. They then returned to the living room. At some point, Towery tried to leave the apartment but Brittany pulled him back in. The evidence also indicated that the two paused during this 45-minute fight, catching their breath and nursing their wounds. Brittany would sustain minor stab wounds to her stomach and thigh.

"This was most likely a fight that had a lot of clutching and grabbing," Orange said. "There was less blood in the living room so the conjecture is that is where the fight started. There was blood near the door so that suggests that Towery was bleeding out and trying to escape for help. Remember, he was a slow-moving 80-year old man. Brittany was a young woman but she was fueled by cocaine. He's getting tired a lot faster than she will."

Eventually, Brittany gained the upper hand. She used various objects around the home to beat down Towery. She started with a cast iron frying pan, then a steam iron, a claw hammer, a fruit knife, a butcher knife and then two forks. Towery would fall to the floor, a bloody mess.

Brittany then took a lamp and shoved its base five inches down his throat which choked him to death.

Satisfied that he had finally killed Tower, Brittany removed her bloody clothes. She washed up in his bathroom then went to his closet to find some clothes that fit her.

Walking back to his dead body, Brittany retrieved the wallet out of Towery's pocket. She took out the $1400 dollars he had and dropped the now empty wallet onto his stomach.

Brittany casually walked out of the apartment and hitched a ride with a young couple. The couple dropped her off at a local crack house where Brittany paid them off with two $100 bills (which had blood stains on them). Inside the drug den, Brittany befriended the proprietor and changed clothes again. She then went to a local hotel with hundreds of dollars worth of cocaine and indulged.

TRIAL

Brittany's defense attorney, Catherine Brown Dodson, would argue that Holberg acted in self-defense when she killed Towery. Her primary argument was that Towery was far from an innocent, elderly man. He was, in fact, a drug abuser himself who became physically violent with Brittany when he found a crack pipe on her person. He then hit Brittany two times in the head when she turned her back to him. Brittany retaliated and ultimately put the lamp post in his mouth in an attempt to end the fight.

Brittany then fled as she believed that no one would believe her side of the story because she was both a prostitute and a drug addict.

While in jail, Brittany would try to coerce Katina Dixon, her cellmate to kill Vickie Marie Kirkpatrick who was the prosecution witness.

Towery's history with prostitutes would be brought up in court testimony. They would also mention incidents of violence with his ex-wife and children but jurors didn't believe the old man was in any type of shape to employ the service of a prostitute.

"My father didn't even like the word 'sex'", one of his sons said. "He was old-fashioned."

A psychiatrist would testify, however, that Brittany had battered wife syndrome, post-traumatic stress disorder, and cocaine addiction.

The jury did not take long to deliberate, finding Brittany to be a cunning, manipulative liar who committed one of the most brutal crimes in the history of Amarillo.

They would find her guilty and Brittany would be moved to death row at Gatesville, Texas.

"I can't even explain to you," Brittany said in a magazine interview. "What it's like to have someone say 'You are sentenced to die.' It's words. You feel helpless, numb. It's almost as if your emotions shut you down."

Brittany would spend her first few weeks in prison laying prone on her bed in a zombie-like state. Over time, she grew accepting of her situation. She knew she was going to die but made it a point to learn to take each day one step at a time.

Her inspiration for cleaning up her act came from the memory of her daughter Mackenzie.

"I cannot live," Brittany said. "And I cannot die, knowing that my child has to live with the horror that these people tried to say about me, the story of the crime, their depiction that I was a cold-blooded person."

Brittany states that she dedicates her days to reading, writing to family and working on her law appeals. She also is anti-death penalty advocate.

She would follow other Texas inmates who were now on death row and make appeals on their behalf, specifically that of Betty Lou Beets.

"I realized," Brittany said. "It doesn't matter whether I'm guilty or innocent, this has now become a very political thing... At this point, they're just killing to kill."

She complained that after a recent jail uprising, the treatment of death row inmates has worsened.

"You would not believe the treatment we are given," Brittany said. "Just two weeks ago, we were informed that not only would we be strip-searched for our one hour of recreation a day, but also when taken for a shower. So for the last two weeks, we have been stripped no less than six times a day. This is every day, sometimes at times like 2:30-3 a.m., and we never leave the building or our cells for that matter."

As of this writing, Brittany's stay of execution has been appealed and appealed for the past eighteen years.

Her attorneys would exhaust the appeal process in the state system but it is now in the federal courts.

Her case, however, has been costing taxpayers "conservatively to be at least $400,000" according to county criminal attorney James Farren. In the future, he has decided to forgo seeking the death penalty in capital cases.

Farren continues to favor a death penalty but only under certain circumstances like "a guy walks into a day care center and kills the children or if someone kills a police officer or a firefighter in the line of duty."

Farren predicted that Brittany would remain on death row for another five years at least. "They can go through the U.S District Court in Amarillo, then it can go to the Fifth U.S Circuit Court and the U.S. Supreme Court. Then from there it can go back to the U.S. District."

But the appeals can come to a halt if the district judge refuses to hear it again.

"If the Supreme Court says 'no'," Farren said. "That's when the district judge can feel safe in stopping this process."

The entire process has been an infuriating one for the Towery family. His son both rages and mourns about what happened to his father.

"She tried to apologize to us during the trial," Russel Towery said. " I got up and walked out. I'm sure other families are going through the same things I'm going through. It's been almost 19 years ... people forget."

"I don't want to die before she does. I want to stand there as she's kicking and screaming going to the death gurney. I want her to think about what my dad went through when she didn't even know his name," he said. "She thinks that because she said she was sorry, that everything's all right. ... she is evil and needs to be destroyed."